Chall–Popp

PHONICS

Level D

1996 REVISION

Jeanne S. Chall, Ph.D. • Helen M. Popp, Ed.D.

 **Continental Press**
Elizabethtown, PA 17022

Project Director:
John F. Onofrey
Interior Illustrations:
Murray Callahan and Ray Burns

ACKNOWLEDGEMENTS

Every effort has been made to trace the ownership of all copyrighted material and to secure the necessary permissions to reprint these selections. In the event of any question arising as to the use of any material, the editor and the publisher, while expressing regret for any inadvertent error, will be happy to make the necessary correction in future printings.

Grateful acknowledgment is made to the following for permission to reprint the copyrighted material listed below.

Dictionary pages

Pages 88, 89, and *92–94:* Dictionary reproductions from *The American Heritage Children's Dictionary.* Copyright © 1986 by Houghton Mifflin Company. Reprinted by permission from *The American Heritage Children's Dictionary.*

Fact sheets

Pages 31–32: "The Shark Lady" adapted from *Ranger Rick* magazine, with permission of the publisher, the National Wildlife Federation. Copyright 1989 NWF.

Pages 59–60: "Winter Sleepers" reprinted from the February 1981 issue of *Ranger Rick* magazine, with permission of the publishers, the National Wildlife Federation. Copyright 1981 by NWF.

Pages 85–86: "The Wolfman" reprinted from the January 1985 issue of *Ranger Rick* magazine, with permission of the publisher, the National Wildlife Federation. Copyright 1985 by NWF.

Pages 125–126: "Boo's World" reprinted from the December 1986 issue of *Ranger Rick* magazine, with permission of the publisher, the National Wildlife Federation. Copyright 1986 by NWF.

Poems

Page 40: "Tea Party" from *Windy Morning* by Harry Behn. Copyright 1953 by Harry Behn. Copyright renewed 1981 by Alice Behn Goebel, Pamela Behn Adam, Prescott Behn, and Peter Behn. Reprinted by permission of Marian Reiner.

Page 40: "Only My Opinion" from *Goose Grass Rhymes* by Monica Shannon. Copyright 1930 by Doubleday, a division of Bantam, Doubleday, Dell Publishing Group, Inc. Used by permission of Doubleday, a division of Bantam Doubleday Dell Publishing Group, Inc.

Page 82: "Stopping by Woods on a Snowy Evening" from *The Poetry of Robert Frost* edited by Edward Connery Lathem. Copyright 1923, © 1969 by Holt, Rinehart and Winston. Copyright 1951 by Robert Frost. Reprinted by permission of Henry Holt and Company, Inc.

Page 106: "Eletelephony" from *Tirra Lirra: Rhymes Old and New* by Laura E. Richards. Copyright 1930, 1932 by Laura E. Richards. Copyright © renewed 1960 by Hamilton Richards. By permission of Little, Brown and Company.

Page 127: "The Library" by Barbara A. Huff from *Random House Book of Poetry for Children* selected by Jack Prelutsky. Copyright 1983. Reprinted by permission of author.

Tales from Around the World

Pages 17–18: "Anansi and the Plantains" from *Anansi the Spiderman* by Philip M. Sherlock. Text © Copyright 1954 by Philip M. Sherlock. Reprinted by permission of HarperCollins Publishers.

Pages 43–44: "Señor Rooster and Señor Fox", a traditional folktale.

Pages 73–74: "The Monkey and the Crocodile" from *Jataka Tales: Animal Stories* by Ellen C. Babbitt. Copyright © 1912, renewed 1940. Prentice Hall, Englewood Cliffs, New Jersey.

Pages 109–110: "Daylight Comes At Last" from *Earthmaker's Tales* by Gretchen Will Mayo. Copyright © 1990 by Gretchen Will Mayo. Reprinted with permission from Walker and Company.

ISBN 0-8454-1248-5

© 1996 The Continental Press, Inc.

C · O · N · T · E · N · T · S

→

C·O·N·T·E·N·T·S

Name _____

Read the selection below. Try to read all the words so you can understand the selection. If you do not know a word, sound the letters and syllables and use other words in the sentences to make a good guess.

Fossils

Fossils are the remains or traces of living things from long ago. They tell the story of dinosaurs and other animals and plants that lived on earth before people did.

Scientists who search for and study fossils are called paleontologists. They find different kinds of fossils. Bones of animals are one kind. Paleontologists have found dinosaur bones over a hundred million years old.

Footprints that were made in mud long ago are also fossils. These tracks were saved when the mud turned to stone.

Stone can hold other kinds of fossils as well, such as the shape of a plant or animal. Perhaps a snail was trapped in mud or clay that hardened. The shell dissolved, but it left a hole, or mold, of its shape in the stone.

Parts of plants or animals that have turned to stone are another kind of fossil. They are called *petrified* fossils. Some petrified tree trunks in the Petrified Forest in Arizona were alive 200 million years ago.

Whole animals are sometimes found, too. Frozen bodies of mammoths that lived over ten thousand years ago were discovered not long ago. They still had their flesh, long wooly hair, and long curving tusks. Mammoths are now extinct. But we know from these fossils that they looked like huge elephants.

Write four difficult words on the lines below.

_____ _____ _____ _____

On the next few pages you will practice short words that will help you read and write the syllables in long words.

Name _____

Circle the word that names the picture. Write it under the picture. Then practice reading all the words as quickly as you can.

bat

pig

sat cap (cat) _cat_	(van) vat vim _van_	
him (hill) ham _hill_	fan cap (can) _can_	(hit) hid hat _hit_
(tip) tad tap _tip_	hit kid (kit) _kit_	dim (dam) dad _dam_
bad bit (bat) _bat_	tab (cad) cab _cad_	rap (rip) rag _rip_
wig (win) wag _win_	(gas) gab sag _gas_	pin pan (pad) _pad_

6   Short vowels in one-syllable words (**a, i**)

Name _____

Write the word that names each picture. It is a one-syllable word.
The vowel letter is either **a** or **i** and has the short sound.

ppin	hat	Babn	leap
ham	Zip	fan	six
suvle	map	pig	Bat
hat	top	Bag	pan

Short vowels in one-syllable words (a, i)

Name _____

Circle the word that names the picture. Write it under the picture. Then practice reading all the words as quickly as you can.

bed

sun

web wit **wet** ⟵ *wet*	rag rug **run** ⟵ *run*
pup pep puff ⟵ *pup*	vat **vet** vest ⟵ *vet*	fill **fell** fed ⟵ *fell*
but beg **bug** ⟵ *bug*	**belt** bend band ⟵ *belt*	bus **sub** sum ⟵ *sub*
hut **hug** hit ⟵ *hug*	malt **melt** mend ⟵ *melt*	**drum** drug drag ⟵ *drum*
bill belt **bell** ⟵ *bell*	**plug** plan plum ⟵ *plug*	jell jut **jet** ⟵ *jell*

8 Short vowels in one-syllable words (**e, u**)

Name _____

Write the word that names each picture. It is a one-syllable word.
The vowel letter is either **e** or **u** and has the short sound.

web	sun	cut	hen
nut	ten	bus	leg
cup	boys	net	tub
Bed	rug	gym	pen

© *The Continental Press, Inc.*

Short vowels in one-syllable words (**e, u**)   **9**

Name _____

Circle the word that names the picture. Write it under the picture. Then practice reading all the words as quickly as you can.

bat   bed

pig

fox   sun

cab		grill	
cob		grin	
cub		grip	
_____		_____	

knit		hit		rod	
kick		hot		red	
king		hut		rid	
_____		_____		_____	

cent		quill	Name Alan	pup	
can't		quiz	1. lid	pep	
cell		quit	2. sand	pop	
			✓3. beng		
			4. mud		
_____		_____		_____	

dill		bunk		pond	
dell		bank		pod	
doll		band		pad	
_____		_____		_____	

swam		dress		skunk	
swing		crop		spunk	
swim		drop		spank	
_____		_____		_____	

Name _____

Write the word that names each picture. It is a one-syllable word.
The vowel letter is **e**, **i**, or **o** and has the short sound.

Name _____

In each box draw lines between two syllables to make four words. Write the words on the lines. Then write the word for the picture on the line below it.

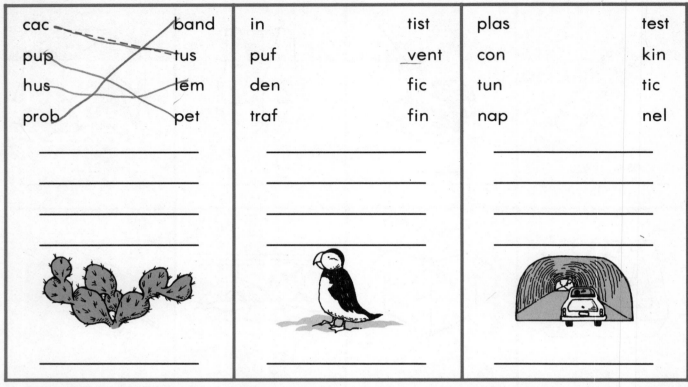

cac	band	in	tist	plas	test
pup	tus	puf	vent	con	kin
hus	lem	den	fic	tun	tic
prob	pet	traf	fin	nap	nel

_____   _____   _____

_____   _____   _____

_____   _____   _____

_____   _____   _____

Read each sentence. Choose a word from above that completes the sentence and write it on the line.

1. There was so much _____ that we could not cross the busy street.

2. Kim won first prize in the art _____ at school.

3. I did not do the last _____ on the math test.

4. If we brush our teeth, the _____ will not have to fill many of them.

5. We buy our milk in a big _____ jug.

6. The men dug a _____ under the road.

7. Ben Franklin wanted to _____ a stove that used less coal, and he did it.

8. Watch out! That _____ plant has sharp spines all over it.

9. My Uncle Dan is Aunt Jane's _____ .

10. The _____ is a big black and white bird with a red and yellow bill.

Name _____

When two consonants come between two vowels, divide the word between the consonants. Try the short sound for the first vowel.

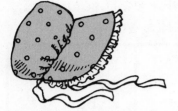   bonnet
         bon   net

   magnet
         mag   net

Divide each word below into two syllables. Write each syllable on a line.

compass   _____ _____   helmet   _____ _____

blanket   _____ _____   pretzel   _____ _____

ribbon   _____ _____   insect   _____ _____

blossoms   _____ _____   cotton   _____ _____

trumpet   _____ _____   pencil   _____ _____

Read each riddle. Choose a word from above that answers the riddle and write it on the line.

1. something that will keep your head safe

_____

2. something most plants have in the spring

_____

3. something you write with

_____

4. something that shows the directions north, east, south, and west

_____

5. something that is an animal with three pairs of legs

_____

6. something you blow into to make music

_____

7. something you put on your bed to keep warm

_____

8. something you tie around a gift

_____

9. something you eat that is salty and has a twisted shape

_____

10. something white and fluffy that grows on a plant

_____

Name _____

Choose the correct word to complete each sentence.
Circle the word and write it in the sentence.

1. Mrs. Hutton makes the best _____ pie.	puppet pumpkin ribbon
2. The children made _____ and ate them in the backyard.	sandboxes sandwiches segments
3. Maria was _____ on the hand by a bug.	bitten button bullet
4. Did you see that fast horse _____ around the track?	gallon gallop gossip
5. After Mike gave a _____, the dog came and sat by his side.	command conduct common
6. We have ten buses in our school _____.	district drastic discuss
7. Our class liked the _____ about the whales.	fifteen flannel filmstrip
8. Three sisters born on the same day are _____.	triplets trumpets picnics
9. Molly and I had corn _____ and milk for a snack.	magnets napkins muffins
10. The _____ of the United States makes laws for our country.	Comment Congress Compass

Name _____

Read the story. Circle the words to complete the sentences.
Write the words in the sentences.

1. The big storm had ended. Our town was under a thick white _____ of snow. School was closed for the day, so I called my pal Tom. "What do you want to do?" I asked.	blanket bandit basket
2. "Let's go skiing at Hobbit Hill," Tom said. "I'll be at your house in a few minutes." After I hung up I went up to the _____ to look for my skis.	album rabbit attic
3. Tom and I hiked over to the ski slope. From the _____ of the hill, it didn't look too bad. But when we got to the top, I felt a bit funny.	bonnet button bottom
4. I had not been skiing for a long time, so Tom gave me a quick _____. Everything was fine. Now I was on my own.	lesson rascal magnet
5. My first downhill run went well. I did not have a _____ staying on my feet.	rotten problem puffin
6. Soon I was racing down the big slope like a speeding _____. The cold wind stung my face.	tunnel bullet pencil
7. There were lots of other skiers on the slope. All of a _____, one of them made a turn in front of me without any warning.	sudden sandal suggest

Reading a story and expressive writing 15

8. I went off the trail so I wouldn't crash into him. Thump! I hit a rock _____ under the snow.	helmet hidden bitten
9. Down I went with a thud. I gave Tom a _____ for help, and he came over to give me a hand.	princess signal sitting
10. "Well," Tom said. "How did this _____? You are lucky that you didn't break any bones."	happen kidnap common
11. The fall had _____ me. But soon I felt like trying the big slope again.	insect puppet upset

Write about something unexpected
that happened to you.

_____

_____

_____

_____

_____

_____

_____

_____

TALES

FROM AROUND THE WORLD

Anansi and the Plantains

It was market day, but Anansi* had no money. He sat at the door of his cottage and watched the other animals hurrying to market. He had nothing to sell, for he had not done any work in his field. How was he to find food for himself, his wife, and his three children?

Soon his wife came to the door and spoke to him. "You must go out, Anansi, and find something for us to eat. We have nothing for lunch and nothing for dinner. What are we going to do without a scrap of food in the house?"

*Anansi: an African folk hero—a spider man

So Anansi helped Rat put the plantains back on his head. Then Anansi set off for home. When he got there, he handed the four plantains to his wife and told her to roast them. He went outside until she called to say that the plantains were ready.

Anansi went back inside. There were the four plantains, nicely roasted. He took one and gave it to the girl. He gave one each to the two boys. He gave the last plantain to his wife. After that he sat down, looking very sad. His wife said to him, "Don't you want some of the plantains?"

"No," said Anansi, with a deep sigh. "There are only enough for four of us."

The little child asked, "Aren't you hungry, Papa?" "Yes, my child, I am hungry, but you are too little. You cannot find food for yourselves. It's better for me to remain hungry as long as your stomachs are filled."

"No, Papa," shouted the children, "you must have half of my plantain." They all broke their plantains in two, and each gave Anansi a half. His wife gave Anansi half of her plantain, too. So, in the end, Anansi got more than anyone, as usual.

"I am going out to work," said Anansi. "Do not worry. Every day you have seen me come home with something. You watch and see!"

Anansi walked about until noon and found nothing, so he lay down under the shade of a large mango tree. There he slept until the sun began to go down. Then he set off for home. He walked slowly, for he was ashamed to go home empty-handed. He asked himself where he would find food for the children. Then he saw his old friend Rat with a large bunch of plantains*. The bunch was so heavy that Rat had to bend over to carry it.

Anansi's eyes shone when he saw the plantains. "How are you, friend Rat? I haven't seen you for a long time."

"Oh, I am staggering along," said Rat. "And how are you—and the family?"

Anansi put on his longest face, so long that his chin almost touched his toes. "Ah, Brother Rat,"

*plantain: a kind of banana

he said, "times are very hard. I can hardly find a thing to eat." Tears came into his eyes.

"I have been walking all day and haven't found a yam or a plantain." Anansi glanced at the large bunch of plantains. "Ah, Br'er Rat, my children will have nothing but water for supper."

"I'm sorry to hear that," said Rat. "I know how I would feel if I had to go home without any food."

"Without even a plantain," said Anansi, and again he looked at the plantains.

Br'er Rat looked at the bunch of plantains, too. He put it on the ground and looked at it in silence. Anansi could not take his eyes away from the plantains. They drew him like a magnet. Rat said nothing. Anansi said nothing.

Then at last Anansi spoke. "My friend," he said, "what a lovely bunch of plantains! Where did you get it in these hard times?"

"It's all that I had left in my field, Anansi. This bunch must last until the peas are ready, and they are not ready yet."

"But they will be ready soon," said Anansi. "Brother Rat, give me one or two of the plantains. The children will have only water for supper."

"All right," said Rat. "Just wait a minute."

Rat counted all the plantains carefully. Finally he broke off the four smallest ones for Anansi.

"Thank you," said Anansi. "But, my friend, you gave me four plantains, and there are five of us."

Rat took no notice of this. He only said, "Help me put this bunch of plantains on my head, Br'er Anansi, and do not try to break off any more."

Name _____

Circle the word that names the picture. Write it under the picture. Then practice reading all the words as quickly as you can.

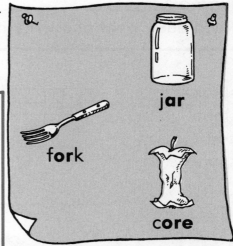

fork

jar

core

star store start	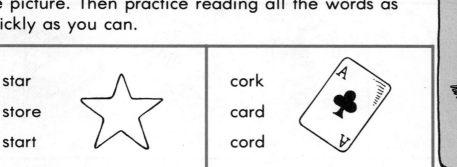	cork card cord	
	_____		_____
can core car		cart corn chore		torch torn tart	
	_____		_____		_____
score scar scrap	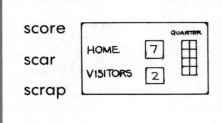	barn bore bar	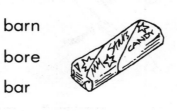	park pork prank	
	_____		_____		_____
born barn barb	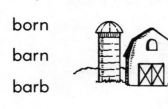	storm stamp store		parch porch port	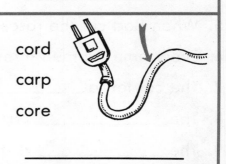
	_____		_____		_____
shore snore shred		frame form farm		cord carp core	
	_____		_____		_____

One-syllable words: vowels with **r** (ar, or, ore)   **19**

Name _____

Read each word and write it under the correct picture.

shark
storm
cart
snore

_____

_____

_____

_____

arm
harp
thorn
yarn

_____

_____

_____

_____

horse
scar
dart
stork

_____

_____

_____

_____

Read each sentence. Write a word from above to complete the sentence.

1. When Frank takes a nap, we can hear him _____.

2. Tammy liked to ride the dark _____ with a star on its chest.

3. The many strings on a _____ make it hard to play.

4. Tina helped her mother push the shopping _____.

5. When Bart cut the roses, he scratched himself on a _____.

6. Every time Carmen threw a _____, it hit its mark.

7. The cut left a _____ on his leg.

8. The _____ has many sharp teeth.

9. The _____ is a bird with long, thin legs.

20   One-syllable words: vowels with **r** (**ar, or, ore**)

Name _____

In each box draw lines between two syllables to make four words. Write the words on the lines. Then write the word for the picture on the line below it.

car	den	plat	vest	tar	ral
doc	sors	hor	cel	cor	get
gar	pet	har	net	mar	bor
scis	tor	par	form	har	ket

_____ _____ _____

_____ _____ _____

_____ _____ _____

_____ _____ _____

_____ _____ _____

Read each riddle. Choose a word from above that answers the riddle and write it on the line.

1. an insect or bug that stings

_____

2. a person who helps the sick

_____

3. a mark to shoot at

_____

4. a package

_____

5. a safe place for ships

_____

6. a place to buy and sell things

_____

7. a place where plants grow

_____

8. a rug

_____

9. a place to keep horses

_____

10. a tool for cutting things

_____

© The Continental Press, Inc.

Name _____

Circle the word that names the picture. Write it under the picture. Then practice reading all the words as quickly as you can.

bird

fern

nurse

grill girl germ	surf scarf sort	
serve verse sort	term torn turn	spark spur spun
harp hard herd	skunk skirt scarf	burst bark burnt
born burn barn	porch purse part	store star stir
third thorn thirst	chirp chip chart	curl curt cart

Name _____

Read each word and write it under the correct picture.

bird
squirt
sharp
fort

_____ _____ _____ _____

twirl
short
clerk
torn

_____ _____ _____ _____

carve
chart
church
fur

_____ _____ _____ _____

Read each sentence. Write a word from above to complete the sentence.

1. Who will _____ the meat for me?

2. Use this tape to mend the _____ page.

3. The _____ did not charge the correct price.

4. The men and horses will be safe inside the _____.

5. The white _____ across from the bank burned down last week.

6. I like a _____ pencil when I write.

7. Please add your name to the _____ on the wall.

8. Josh is too _____ to reach the top shelf.

9. Many people think it is wrong to kill animals for their _____.

One-syllable words: vowels with **r** (**ar, or, er, ir, ur**)

Name _____

When two consonants come between two vowels, divide the word into syllables between them. If either syllable ends in the letter **r**, try the **r**-sound for the vowel.

 mirror

mir   ror

 hammer

ham   mer

Divide each word below into two syllables. Write each syllable on a line.

serpent _____ _____   circus _____ _____

lantern _____ _____   forgot _____ _____

hermit _____ _____   perfect _____ _____

gerbils _____ _____   barber _____ _____

support _____ _____   chapter _____ _____

Read each sentence. Choose a word from above that completes the sentence and write it on the line.

1. Did you read the last _____ in the book?

2. Beth held the _____ so we could see in the dark cave.

3. The shelf will not _____ all those books.

4. The _____ lived alone in a small house in the woods.

5. The _____ cut my hair too short.

6. The animals in the _____ are well trained.

7. It was a _____ day to take a plane ride.

8. I _____ to put a stamp on that letter.

9. A large snake may be called a _____.

10. Most _____ eat, play, and sleep in a cage.

Name _____

Read the four headings in each column. Then read the words at the top of the column. Write each word under its correct heading.

rancher	hammer	otter
muskrat	shirt	actor
slippers	bobcat	drill
fork	shepherd	scarf

Animals

_____

_____

_____

Tools

_____

_____

_____

Things to Wear

_____

_____

_____

Persons

_____

_____

_____

Vermont	pretzel	organ
buzzard	horn	Wisconsin
cherry	Kansas	trumpet
blackbird	turnip	puffin

States

_____

_____

_____

Birds

_____

_____

_____

Things to Eat

_____

_____

_____

Things That Make Music

_____

_____

_____

Name _____

The letter **y** at the end of a one-syllable word often stands for the long **i** sound.

y = i
fl**y**

The letter **y** at the end of a word with more than one syllable often stands for the long **e** sound.

y = e
penn**y**

Read each word and write it under the correct picture.

spy
buggy
berry
fifty

_____   _____   _____   _____

fry
windy
daisy
cry

_____   _____   _____   _____

Read each sentence. Write a word from above to complete the sentence.

1. The stars on our flag stand for the _____ states in our country.

2. The _____ had hidden the plans under the porch.

3. The hornet sting hurt so much that it made me _____.

4. Dad likes to _____ fish over a campfire.

5. I can eat _____ shortcake anytime, can't you?

6. You need a _____ day to fly a kite.

7. The pretty white _____ had a yellow center.

8. A horse and _____ used to be a good way to get places.

Name _____

Read each riddle. Choose the correct word from the box and write it on the line below the riddle.

poppy   ferry   fancy
      dry
 city   jelly
     forty
	candy sly sky
	     sloppy
	 shy story
	     empty

1. This word means the opposite of **plain**.

_____

2. This is a boat that can carry people and cars.

_____

3. This flower can be red or orange.

_____

4. This word means the opposite of **wet**.

_____

5. This is something you put on bread.

_____

6. This is a big place where many people live and work.

_____

7. This number comes after thirty-nine.

_____

8. This is something you read in a book.

_____

9. This is something sweet to eat.

_____

10. This word means the opposite of **neat**.

_____

11. This is always above us.

_____

12. This word means the same as **clever** or **tricky**.

_____

13. This word means the opposite of **full**.

_____

14. This word means the same as **bashful**.

_____

September

The goldenrod is yellow;
　　The corn is turning brown;
The trees in apple orchards
　　With fruit are bending down.

The gentian's bluest fringes
　　Are curling in the sun;
In dusty pods the milkweed
　　Its hidden silk has spun.

The sedges flaunt their harvest
　　In every meadow nook;
And asters by the brook-side
　　Make asters in the brook.

From dewy lanes at morning
　　The grapes' sweet odors rise;
At noon the roads all flutter
　　With yellow butterflies.

By all these lovely tokens
　　September days are here,
With summer's best of weather,
　　And autumn's best of cheer.

Helen Hunt Jackson

Name _____

Read the story. Circle the words to complete the sentences.
Write the words in the sentences.

1. My name is Jane Karp. Of all the _____ at school, I like soccer best. A soccer team has 10 players and a goalie. Our team is very good at kicking and passing the ball.	starts sports charts
2. The players try to get the ball past the other team's goalie and across the goal line. A net is fastened to a _____ between two posts in back of the goal line.	cranberry crossword crossbar
3. Last week we played Camden on a wet field. It was hard to hit the slippery ball. You can hit it with any part of your body _____ your hands and arms.	success express except
4. Camden got off to a fast start. They scored a goal right away and took the lead. Our team had to kick against a strong wind in the _____ half of the game.	fresh firm first
5. One of Camden's players hit the ball with her _____, and the wind took it into the net. At halftime Camden was ahead 2–0.	forehead forest firefly
6. Then Jill Hanson on our team kicked the ball high into the air. The ball dropped inside the left _____ of the net. The first goal for our team!	camper corner cracker
7. No one seemed to be able to make a goal after that. Both goalies made save after save. They did not _____ to let a ball get past the goal line. The scored stayed at 2–1.	infect intend discuss

8. At last the best _____ of our team sent that muddy ball rolling hard. It zipped past the Camden goalie and went right into one corner of the net.	month murmur member
9. Now the score was tied, 2–2. Both teams played hard as the minutes ticked by. I hit the ball off the inside of my foot and watched it _____ around into the net. A goal!	curve cord crisp
10. We had to keep Camden from scoring. With 20 seconds left, Camden's _____ 17 made a super kick. The ball went high into the air.	Northern Number Mustard
11. It hit the crossbar and bounced down outside the goal line. The game was over. We had won, 3–2! What a _____ break for us!	leaky locker lucky

Write about a game that your team won.

_____

_____

_____

_____

_____

_____

_____

_____

The Shark Lady Eugenie Clark

Eugenie rides a whale shark down into the ocean depths.

Down...down...down, into the cold, dark ocean depths, glides a huge whale shark. On the shark's back rides a small, dark-haired woman. She is Eugenie Clark, "The Shark Lady."

Eugenie holds tight to the shark's big back fin. Down the two go...100...130...150 feet.

"That was one of those times when I wished I were a fish," Eugenie said later. "Then I could go wherever they go."

Eugenie has been hooked on fish since she was a child. She spent hours with her nose pressed against the tanks in the New York City Aquarium. When she was in college, she put on her first diving mask and flippers. She dove into the sea, where the fish live free, and she studied about them. She learned enough to become *Doctor* Clark, an expert fish biologist.

How to Meet a Shark

To Eugenie, there's nothing more wonderful than swimming underwater for hours, nose-to-nose with angelfish and eels, octopuses and...sharks!

Dr. Clark enjoys swimming with eels and octopuses.

Eugenie says sharks aren't "mean," as many people believe. They attack only to eat or because they feel afraid. Eugenie is very careful in the water. She doesn't see why *anyone* who is diving carefully should be afraid.

"You just have to realize that you are a visitor in the fish's backyard," she says.

Eugenie met her first big shark when she was swimming near a coral reef. A shark came straight toward her. It was so close she could have reached out and touched it. But she didn't. She just stayed perfectly still and stared, unafraid. All Eugenie could think was, *How lucky I am to see that sleek, beautiful creature so close up!*

After that, Eugenie met lots of sharks face to face. Once she spent ten days observing great white sharks from a metal diving cage. Her first moments underwater with the giant fish were unforgettable. One shark came straight at the cage with its mouth open so wide that Eugenie could see right down its throat. As the shark's jaws crunched down on the cage, its nose poked through the space between the bars. Eugenie pressed her body against the opposite side of the cage. But at the same time, another shark swam by and brushed against her back!

A great white shark tries to eat Eugenie's cage.

Sharks with "Smarts"

Sharks, everybody once thought, were not only mean, but stupid too.

That was before Eugenie proved what sharks can learn. At her marine laboratory, three sharks were taught to press a target to get food. They even learned to tell white targets from red, and striped ones from plain-colored ones.

Eugenie discovered that sharks can remember things too. After *not* working with the targets for two months, the sharks went right back to pressing targets for their food again—just as if they had been doing it every day.

The Shark's Best Friend

Eugenie believes that the more we know about sharks, the less we'll fear them. By writing her books and articles, teaching, making films, and giving talks, Eugenie spreads the word about sharks. She wants everyone to know what she knows: Sharks are magnificent animals that deserve respect, not fear.

 ## Bookshelf

These books will tell you more about sharks.

Anton, Tina. *Sharks, Sharks, Sharks.* Milwaukee, Wisc.: Raintree, 1989.

McGovern, Ann. *Shark Lady.* New York: Scholastic, 1987.

Maestro, Betsy. *A Sea Full of Sharks.* New York: Scholastic, 1990.

Name _____

Listen to each word. Find the word in the box and circle it.

1.	2.	3.	4.	5.
bullet	index	gusher	bantam	pollen
belfry	onset	gospel	bandit	pencil
ballot	annex	midship	bonnet	pompom
bolster	indent	gossip	summit	pulpit

6.	7.	8.	9.	10.
gunshot	extinct	citrus	funnel	mussel
bucket	express	circus	furnace	muskrat
buckskin	extend	census	fungus	musket
buckshot	undress	center	cactus	mistress

11.	12.	13.	14.	15.
carton	tidbit	actress	parcel	burden
cotton	trumpet	anklet	percent	burner
correct	timber	enter	perfect	butter
carbon	tinker	actor	person	burlap

16.	17.	18.	19.	20.
furthest	error	expert	whirlwind	mirror
furlong	orbit	adore	warning	murder
farther	organ	ignore	whisker	mortar
furnish	order	escort	whisper	murmur

21.	22.	23.	24.	25.
granny	cry	entry	simple	spry
grizzly	classy	ugly	crisply	supply
grassy	clothes	try	simply	sentry
grubby	clumsy	pantry	simmer	wry

Review for Units 1 and 2   **33**

Name _____

When a word has only one consonant between two vowels, divide the word after the first vowel and try the long sound of that vowel.

robot

ro   bot

Divide each word into two syllables and write them on the lines.

cement _____ _____   tiger _____ _____

spider _____ _____   pupil _____ _____

flavor _____ _____   omit   _____ _____

protect _____ _____   pilot _____ _____

clover _____ _____   hotel _____ _____

Read each riddle. Choose a word from above that answers the riddle and write it on the line.

1. The taste and smell of food in your mouth is its _____.

2. If you leave something out, you _____ it.

3. You mix _____ with water and use it to make sidewalks.

4. The part of your eye that lets the light in is the _____.

5. When you keep animals safe from harm, you _____ them.

6. _____ is a plant with leaves that have three parts.

7. A _____ is a place where you can rent a room for a few days.

8. An animal that spins a web to catch insects is a _____.

9. A person who can fly an airplane is a _____.

10. The _____ is a large animal in the cat family with black stripes on its orange coat.

Name _____

When a word has only one consonant between two vowels, divide it after the first vowel and try the long sound of that vowel.

robot
ro   bot

When the long vowel sound in the first syllable does not make a word, divide the word after the consonant and try the short sound of the vowel.

robin
rob   in

Divide each word into two syllables and write them on the lines.

fever	_____	_____	model	_____	_____
radar	_____	_____	legend	_____	_____
gravy	_____	_____	camel	_____	_____
solar	_____	_____	lizard	_____	_____
driver	_____	_____	solid	_____	_____

Read each sentence. Choose a word from above that completes the sentence and write it on the line.

1. Sam made a _____ of the racing car he liked.

2. Everyone blames the accident on the _____ of the bus.

3. A small animal with four legs, scaly skin, and a long tail is a _____.

4. In science class we learn that you can change ice from a _____ to a liquid, and then to a gas.

5. If you are very sick and feel hot, you may have a _____.

6. The energy we get from the sun is called _____ energy.

7. Do you believe the _____ of Paul Bunyan and his blue ox?

8. The hump on the back of a _____ is muscle and fat.

9. Many ships and planes use _____ to guide them through storms and fog.

10. I like my mashed potatoes with lots of _____.

Name _____

Read the selection below. If you do not know the underlined words, remember: When a word has only one consonant between two vowels, divide it after the first vowel and try the long sound of that vowel. If that does not make a word, divide the word after the consonant and try the short sound of the vowel.

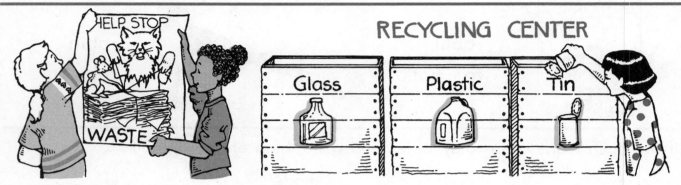

In <u>modern</u> times we use many things only once and then throw them away. How many <u>items</u> did you throw away at your house this week?

How can we save our <u>planet</u> so it does not become a huge pile of trash? We must find ways to <u>prevent</u> waste. We must all <u>begin</u> to work hard and change our bad <u>habits</u>.

At school we are working on a <u>project</u> about waste. Some <u>students</u> are using their <u>talents</u> to make posters. Janet and Helen did a <u>comic</u> sketch of

a <u>timid</u> mouse helping a fox tie up <u>papers</u>.

Peter and Jason set up huge bins at school. Each bin has a big <u>label</u> on it—glass, tin, or plastic. In this way <u>pupils</u> can recycle bottles and cans.

The <u>local</u> paper had a story on its front page about our project. The report said our class was doing a splendid job and gave us lots of <u>credit</u>. But it is up to everyone to make the project a success.

Divide the underlined words above and write them in the correct column below. Write the words with a long vowel sound in the first syllable under **robot**. Write the words with a short vowel sound in the first syllable under **robin**.

robot

1. _____ _____   5. _____ _____

2. _____ _____   6. _____ _____

3. _____ _____   7. _____ _____

4. _____ _____   8. _____ _____

robin

1. _____ _____   5. _____ _____

2. _____ _____   6. _____ _____

3. _____ _____   7. _____ _____

4. _____ _____   8. _____ _____

Name _____

When a word ends in a consonant plus **le**, divide the word before that consonant. If the first syllable ends in a consonant, try the short sound of the vowel. If the first syllable ends with a vowel, try the long sound of the vowel.

 bubble

bub ble

 table

ta ble

Change only one letter in each word to make a new word that fits the meaning.

1. Change **tumble** to a word that means "a deep rolling sound." _____ *rumble*_____

2. Change **jungle** to a word that means "to make a ringing sound." _____ *jingle*_____

3. Change **paddle** to a word for "a small pool of water." _____

4. Change **middle** to a word for a question that puzzles you. _____

5. Change **battle** to a word for large animals such as cows and oxen. _____

6. Change **cable** to a word for a story that tells a lesson. _____

7. Change **mumble** to a word for a sudden fall. _____

8. Change **thistle** to a word for something you blow into to make a high sound. _____

9. Change **bottle** to a word that means a fight, often in a war. _____

10. Change **giggles** to a word for a pair of glasses to protect your eyes from wind, water, dust, sun, or sparks. _____

11. Change **tingle** to a word that means "the only one." _____

12. Change **candle** to a word for the part of a door that you pull or push to open it. _____

13. Change **saddle** to a word for a short oar that is used to move a boat through the water. _____

14. Change **cattle** to a word for a baby's toy that makes noise. _____

Puzzle page: two-syllable words ending in **Cle** **37**

Name _____

Choose the correct word to complete each sentence.
Circle the word and write it in the sentence.

1. When water boils, it gets very hot and _____.	bundles bubbles battles
2. Papa asked me to sit still when he cut my hair. "You _____ like a little worm," he said.	quarrel drizzle wiggle
3. Our class watched TV and saw the space _____ land in the desert.	shuttle shuffle sparkle
4. Have you ever played a game with little round glass balls that are called _____?	mumbles marbles markers
5. We see many more shows since we have _____ TV.	cackle cable castle
6. That book has an interesting _____. I think it will be fun to read about "The Shark Lady."	title turtle tumble
7. Sap from the _____ tree can be boiled and made into a sweet syrup.	maple middle mingle
8. Marcus played the _____ at camp to wake us up.	gurgle purple bugle
9. My pet rabbit likes to _____ on carrots.	ripple nibble nozzle
10. How did Min happen to twist her _____ on that short hike?	ankle uncle angle

Name _____

Read each definition and write a word for it in the letter spaces. The first letters of the words are written in for you. Use your dictionary if you need help to spell the words correctly.

1. to shake, sometimes because you're cold
2. a make-believe beast
3. a waterway that joins two bodies of water
4. a small yellow fruit that tastes sour
5. to go to see someone or something
6. to trip and almost fall
7. a place which is larger than a town

8. to touch someone lightly and make them laugh
9. the number after six

10. the sum we get by adding numbers
11. to rub something to make it shine
12. a fruit that is often used to make pies

13. a small, simple house often made of logs
14. a bed for a little baby
15. a time, at school, to relax and have fun
16. a land and water animal with a hard shell

17. the color you get when you mix red and blue
18. another word for a smell
19. a round shape
20. a stream of water that is larger than a brook
21. the seed of an oak tree
22. the seventh month of the year

Read down from the star to get the message:

"_____ ____ ____ _____ _____."

Is it true? _____

Tea Party

Mister Beedle Baddlebug,
Don't bandle up in your boodlebag
Or numble in your jumblejug,
Now eat your nummy tiffletag
Or I will never invite you
To tea again with me. Shoo!

Harry Behn

Only My Opinion

Is a caterpillar ticklish?
  Well, it's always my belief
That he giggles, as he wiggles
  Across a hairy leaf.

Monica Shannon

Name _____

Read the story. Circle the words to complete the sentences.
Write the words in the sentences.

1. All over Germany people were talking about Mr. Von Osten and his wonderful horse, Hans. Hans could tap his hoof and answer math problems. He was a _____ horse.	clever closet clover
2. Not everyone believed that an animal could solve math problems. The _____ people of the town and visitors from far away came to see for themselves.	label local limit
3. They came to see Hans perform in the _____ of the courtyard. A man asked Mr. Von Osten if Hans could answer problems he had not worked on ahead of time.	melon middle music
4. The man's question upset Mr. Von Osten, but he calmly asked the man to give Hans a problem himself. The man did not give a _____ problem.	saddle simple shingle
5. The man said, "If I add 3 to a number and multiply it by 4, I get 28. What number am I thinking of?" No words were _____ to give the answer to the horse.	spider sprinkle spoken
6. The problem did not seem to _____ clever Hans. He tapped his hoof 1, 2, 3, 4 times and stopped. Could a horse really be that smart?	puzzle pupil purple
7. Day after day Hans tapped out correct answers. But it was a _____ for some people to believe that Hans really knew the answers to these problems.	smuggle struggle strangle

8. Men came from the university to _____ Hans and his owner. Each day they kept an eye on Mr. Von Osten's head, eyes, hands, and even his feet, looking for clues.	spirit student study
9. None of them could see any secret signals being given. They gave Hans problems themselves. Perhaps the _____ was true. Maybe Hans really could solve problems.	rumor ruler relax
10. Then they began to notice something about Hans. He was _____ to answer the problem only when he could look at a person who knew the answer.	angle able actor
11. People did not know themselves that they were giving tiny signals that Hans could see. That's how Hans knew the right _____ to stop tapping. Clever Hans!	modern manner moment

Write about a clever animal you have seen.

_____

_____

_____

_____

_____

_____

_____

_____

TALES
FROM AROUND THE WORLD

Señor Rooster and Señor Fox

Señor Rooster was a fine bird and a smart one, too. He liked to take walks beyond the village to see the world.

One day he took a long walk and wandered deep into the forest. He came to a tall tree and decided to fly high up into the branches and look at the whole world from there.

Now Señor Fox came walking through the woods. As he passed under the tree, he heard Señor Rooster flapping his wings in the branches. He saw the feathers of Señor Rooster and his fat body. "What a fine dinner Señor Rooster would make," he thought. But Señor Fox had no wings

"From which direction are they coming? Please tell me quickly! From where?"

"They're coming from over that way," said Señor Rooster. He pointed with his wing in exactly the opposite direction from which he saw them.

"I'd better run along now," cried Señor Fox. I'm in a hurry." And off he ran, as fast as his legs would carry him.

"Señor Fox! Señor Fox!" called Señor Rooster. "Don't run away! Don't go! You can tell the dogs and the hunter about the new law among the animals in the forest."

Señor Fox ran into the dogs, and Señor Rooster sat in the tree.

If you dig a pit to catch someone innocent, you often fall into it yourself. Being too smart is bad luck.

and could not fly up into the tree. Nor could he climb. Well, he remembered that good words often pave good roads.

"My dear, dear friend, Señor Rooster!" Señor Fox cried. "How are you today? It seems very strange for a famous gentleman like you to be all alone. I'm sure all the fine hens in the henhouse are worried about you. They are wondering where you have gone."

"Good Señor Fox," replied Señor Rooster, "just let them wait. The longer they wait, the happier they will be to see me when I return."

"You're a smart gentleman, Señor Rooster, and very wise. But I wouldn't let the poor hens wait too long. Come down and we'll walk together to the henhouse. I'm going that way."

"Ha, ha, ha!" laughed the rooster. "What sweet words you use to catch me! Do you really think I'll come down so you can make a good dinner of me? Sweet words catch fools."

"Don't say that, Señor Rooster. Maybe in my former days I was guilty of such things, but no more. Besides, haven't you heard about the new law in the forest? No animal can eat another; all are to be friends. Anyone who breaks the new law will be punished. I'm surprised you haven't heard about it. Everyone knows it."

"Well, that's news to me, Señor Fox."

"I wouldn't dare to eat you now, even if I were starving to death. Honestly. On my honor."

"Well, it must be true, when you talk like that," said Señor Rooster.

"It's the absolute truth, Señor Rooster. So you see, you can come down now."

"Really!" said Señor Rooster, but still he did not come down. Instead, he looked around in all directions. Suddenly he saw a hunter approaching with his dogs. That gave him an idea. He began to count slowly: "One... two... three... four...."

"What are you counting, good friend Rooster?"

"Five... six...."

"What are you counting? Tell me, friend."

Señor Rooster pretended he hadn't heard, and said, "Six fine, big hunting dogs running this way, and a man with a gun behind them!"

"Dogs! What dogs? Coming this way? With a hunter?"

"Yes, Señor Fox, all coming this way!"

Name _____

Listen to each word. Find the word in the box and circle it.

1.	2.	3.	4.	5.
clothes	limit	metal	moment	recess
closet	linen	melted	modern	rakes
close	lime	miller	muddy	ruler
classic	limping	melon	medal	relax

6.	7.	8.	9.	10.
stutter	sister	bacon	disgust	bison
student	circle	backbone	ditches	bicycle
stumble	civil	bakery	digger	bishop
stooped	silver	basket	digit	bitten

11.	12.	13.	14.	15.
fable	humble	lesson	metal	petal
favor	humming	leaving	mitten	pity
factory	humor	level	method	pistil
fabric	hunger	legal	meter	petted

16.	17.	18.	19.	20.
baffle	cable	giggle	maple	nipple
bundle	cuddle	gentle	nibble	nozzle
battle	cradle	gurgle	noble	muzzle
bubble	cripple	grumble	knuckle	marble

21.	22.	23.	24.	25.
riddle	sample	ruffle	uncle	sparkle
rumble	stable	stumble	bugle	freckle
purple	struggle	shingle	idle	sprinkle
ripple	scramble	shuffle	able	speckle

Name _____

Read the selection below. Try to read all the words so you can understand the selection. If you do not know a word, sound the letters and syllables and use other words in the sentences to make a good guess.

Do Animals Use Tools?

Scientists used to think that only humans used tools. Now they know better. Sea otters, birds, chimpanzees, and elephants are among the animals that have been observed using tools.

It is amazing to see the way a sea otter uses a stone as a tool. The otter floats on its back and holds a stone on its chest. Then it bangs a shellfish against the stone, trying to break the shell. After many blows, the shell breaks and the otter eats the flesh inside.

In South America, the woodpecker finch uses a twig as a tool. It holds a twig in its beak to push insects out of cracks in the bark of trees.

Jane Goodall watched with great excitement as a chimpanzee used a stem of grass as a tool. The chimp poked the stem into a termite nest and then pulled it out. The stem was full of termites that the chimp ate.

Elephants are also tool users. They have been seen in the wild using sticks to scratch themselves. This use of a stick to achieve a goal is another example of an animal using a tool.

Humans are the best tool makers and users. But other creatures also use tools to produce results.

Write four difficult words on the lines below.

_____ _____ _____ _____

On the next few pages you will practice short words that will help you read and write the syllables in long words.

Name _____

Circle the word that names the picture. Write it under the picture. Then practice reading all the words as quickly as you can.

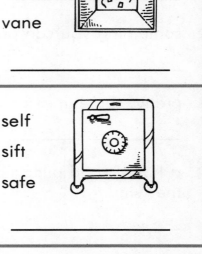

can   cane

kit   kite

fact face fate _____	dime dim dive _____	
cage cap cape _____	twine tame twin _____	flick flake flack _____
strike strip stripe _____	shift save shave _____	fire fry fir _____
bird bride burn _____	dike dice dig _____	from frame vane _____
scale sketch skate _____	hive hate hit _____	self sift safe _____

One-syllable words: short and long **a** and **i** (CVC and CVCe)

Name _____

| rob | robe | cub | cube |

Read each word and write it under the correct picture.

code
cut
cone
cute

B = 1   N = 5
E = 2   P = 6
H = 3   R = 7
L = 4   T = 8

$\overline{3}\ \overline{2}\ \overline{4}\ \overline{6}$

_____ _____ _____

dome
dune
doll
dump

_____ _____ _____ _____

Read each riddle. Choose a word that answers the riddle and write it on the line.

1. a large round roof

_____

2. something you can put ice cream in

_____

3. pretty, sometimes clever

_____

4. a hill of sand piled up by the wind

_____

5. to unload or let fall in a heap

_____

6. a toy that looks like a person

_____

7. a set of signals to send a message

_____

8. to divide with something sharp, as a knife

_____

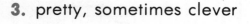

Name _____

In each box draw lines between two syllables to make four words. Write the words on the lines. Then write the word for the picture on the line below it.

cup	change	de	takes	grape	plore
ex	bone	mis	pire	pro	mire
trom	cate	um	vice	ex	vines
lo	cakes	ad	scribe	ad	vide

_____   _____   _____

_____   _____   _____

_____   _____   _____

_____   _____   _____

_____   _____   _____

Read each sentence. Choose a word from above that completes the sentence and write it on the line.

1. Ted wants to _____ his new shirt for a larger size.

2. Shana made two _____ on her math test.

3. Our artwork is very good. You will _____ all of it.

4. Take my _____ and do not stay in the sun too long.

5. The fans did not think the _____ made a fair call in the last inning of the baseball game.

6. Mom will bake plenty of _____ for the school party.

7. President Jefferson asked Lewis and Clark to _____ the Far West.

8. The _____ is my favorite musical instrument.

9. How can we _____ shelter for people who do not have a home?

10. Can you _____ the Mississippi River on a map of the United States?

Name _____

When a syllable has a consonant and final **e** following the vowel, try the long sound for that vowel.

trom   bone
trombone

re   cite
recite

Divide each word into two syllables and write them on the lines.

tadpole _____ _____   refuse _____ _____

stampede _____ _____   cyclone _____ _____

costume _____ _____   erase _____ _____

reptile _____ _____   prepare _____ _____

surprise _____ _____   decide _____ _____

Read each riddle. Choose a word from above that answers the riddle and write it on the line.

1. something that is not expected or that happens suddenly

   _____

2. something worn by an actor in a play

   _____

3. to say "no" to someone

   _____

4. a windstorm—similar to a tornado

   _____

5. something that hatches from the egg of a frog

   _____

6. to rub something out, like a mistake

   _____

7. an animal like a snake or lizard whose skin is often covered with scales

   _____

8. to get ready for something or someone

   _____

9. a sudden rush of many animals

   _____

10. to make up your mind about something

   _____

Choose the correct word to complete each sentence.
Circle the word and write it in the sentence.

1. Let's look at a map and _____ the size of Texas with the size of Delaware.		compete compare concern
2. Cindy asked her teacher to _____ the spelling words more slowly.		dictate describe decade
3. I hope Mrs. Davis will _____ me from class so I can go to the dentist.		excuse explore extreme
4. Were you able to _____ the crossword puzzle?		complete comfort concrete
5. If our team wins this game, I _____ we will go to the state playoffs.		sincere suppose supreme
6. The scent from the flowers in the garden was like _____ .		perfume perform polite
7. Kelly _____ as soon as the sun began to shine in her window.		erase arose advise
8. You are trying to mix me up. Why do you want to _____ me?		current connect confuse
9. They will construct a _____ from one end of the state to the other.		transfer turnpike traffic
10. The men and women in the space _____ will orbit the earth for several weeks.		capsule compose compare

© The Continental Press, Inc. Reading sentences: two-syllable words ending with long vowels **51**

Name _____

Circle the word that names the picture. Write it under the picture. Then practice reading all the words as quickly as you can.

n**ai**l

tr**ay**

b**oa**t

chin claim chain _____	soap soak sap _____
jail jay jar _____	hail hand hay _____
faint float flock _____	tide tail toad _____
play plan loan _____	spank spray sprain _____
paint part pray _____	taste toast tail _____

snail <br> snake <br> sail
 _____

main <br> mile <br> mail
 _____

coat <br> coach <br> chat
 _____

pail <br> poach <br> plant
 _____

52   One-syllable words: vowel digraphs **ai**, **ay**, and **oa**

Name _____

In each box draw lines between two syllables to make four words. Write the words on the lines. Then write the word for the picture on the line below it.

up	plain	rail	day	a	dream
sail	stairs	dis	coal	mail	box
drive	boat	Thurs	road	day	ty
ex	way	char	play	dain	wait

_____

_____

_____

_____

_____

_____

_____

_____

_____

_____

_____

_____

Read each sentence. Choose a word from above that completes the sentence and write it on the line.

1. Can you _____ what happens when a star explodes?

2. The post office collects letters from this _____ each night.

3. It was too windy to take the _____ out of the harbor.

4. My sister always slept _____ in the attic at grandma's house.

5. We made a _____ fire and roasted hot dogs over it.

6. I hope the art teacher will _____ our paintings where our parents will see them.

7. Dad's car is in the garage, so put your bikes in our _____.

8. The butterfly is a _____ insect with lacy wings.

9. My class will go to the library on _____.

10. In 1869 the U.S. had its first _____ line that went from coast to coast.

Name _____

queen

leaf

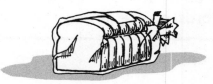

bread

Read each word and write it under the correct picture.

screen
steam
heel
head

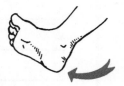

_____ _____ _____ _____

beast
beach
thread
cheek

_____ _____ _____ _____

Read each riddle. Choose a word that answers the riddle and write it on the line.

1. a large animal with four feet

    _____

2. the back part of your shoe

    _____

3. what water turns into when it gets very hot

    _____

4. you have one of these on each side of your face, under your eyes

    _____

5. a fine, thin cord, used with a needle

    _____

6. this keeps insects out of our homes

    _____

7. a sandy place where water and land meet

    _____

8. your brain is in this part of your body

    _____

Name _____

If a syllable has a vowel digraph, try the sound those letters stand for.

te   pee   sweat   band   sea   plane
tepee   sweatband   seaplane

Divide each word below into two syllables. Write each syllable on a line.

breakfast   _____ _____   canteen   _____ _____

beehive   _____ _____   forehead   _____ _____

weekend   _____ _____   repeat   _____ _____

teamwork   _____ _____   seaweed   _____ _____

fifteen   _____ _____   treaty   _____ _____

Read each sentence. Choose a word from above that completes the sentence and write it on the line.

1. The baseball coach thinks we can win the pennant this year with our good _____ .

2. Do you eat a good _____ every morning?

3. Many kinds of _____ grow in the sea.

4. On the hike, we will carry drinking water in a _____ .

5. After the war ends, the two leaders will sign a peace _____ .

6. If you are nine years old, you will be _____ in six years.

7. When Monday arrives, the _____ is over.

8. The students asked the teacher to _____ the math problem.

9. That clown always paints red and white stripes on her _____ .

10. Bees can tell each other how far it is from their _____ to where they gather nectar.

Two-syllable words: vowel digraphs **ee** and **ea**

Name _____

Choose the correct word to complete each sentence.
Circle the word and write it in the sentence.

1. The four _____ of the year are spring, summer, fall, and winter.	meetings seasons servants
2. The enemy began to _____ when they saw the size of our army.	reason retreat rotate
3. If today is Monday, then _____ was Sunday.	weekday yesterday Friday
4. A sunny day is perfect _____ for a boat trip down the river.	weather weapon weeping
5. How many quarts of milk does a gallon _____ ?	contain cardboard contest
6. When Estelle let the mice out of their cage, it caused an _____ in the classroom.	ideal upland uproar
7. It was a surprise to learn Julio was sick because he looked so _____ .	healthy heavy heaven
8. The sailor told a story about a _____ with long, golden hair and a silver tail.	weary mermaid meanwhile
9. In the play Nancy will _____ as a mad monster.	appear accuse arrange
10. The children were waiting to see who would _____ them at Fernando's party.	entertain raindrop remain

Reading sentences: two-syllable words with vowel digraphs

Name _____

Read the story. Circle the words to complete the sentences.
Write the words in the sentences.

1. Plastics in the ocean are a threat to mammals, fish, and birds. They cause the death of thousands of sea _____ each year.	creatures costumes parades
2. Small whales and seals often get tangled up in huge plastic fishing nets that stretch for miles. The animals cannot _____, and they drown.	feather estate escape
3. Sea turtles often _____ floating plastic bags for jellyfish, their favorite food.	succeed mistake trapeze
4. The turtles eat the plastic bags and may choke on them. It is a _____ death for the turtles.	peanut painful figure
5. Sometimes a factory dumps little pieces of plastic into rivers and streams. As these plastic pellets make their way to the sea, they can be _____ to many animals.	admire dairy deadly
6. The plastic pellets look like little crabs and shrimp to a mother _____. She feeds them to her babies, or nestlings. The pellets get stuck in their throats and they cannot breathe.	seabird subway tailor
7. Every day about 640,000 plastic _____ are dumped overboard. Millions of pounds of plastic fishing lines and nets are lost or dumped at sea each year.	empires excuses containers

Reading a story and expressive writing **57**

8. Plastics are strong and do not break down or decay. They do not disintegrate [dis-in-te-grate]. Plastics can _____ harmful for a very long time.	awake remain amaze
9. We need to _____ ways to solve this problem. New kinds of plastics that can disintegrate are being developed and used.	expert explore decade
10. In 1989 Congress passed a law to stop the dumping of plastics in the ocean. Now fishermen must _____ to stop using huge plastic fishing nets near places where birds nest.	degree awhile agree
11. We can also help. What would happen if each of us began to recycle plastics _____ of dumping them?	instead injure explain

Write a story about a baby seal
that gets trapped in a fishing net.

_____

_____

_____

_____

_____

_____

_____

Winter Sleepers

Ground squirrels dig special rooms for their long winter sleep.

Did you turn down the thermostat in your house this winter to save energy? Animals such as woodchucks, bats, and ground squirrels have been turning down their "thermostats" for years! You can't find thermostats on the walls of their dens or burrows. Instead, their "thermostats" are inside their bodies. They turn them down before cold weather comes, when they go into a very deep sleep called *hibernation*.

Hibernation

When an animal starts to hibernate, strange things happen. Its heartbeat slows way down, and it hardly breathes. Its body temperature may drop to just above freezing! The animal seems to be near death. When its "thermostat" is turned down this way, it needs very little energy to stay alive. The animal lives on the extra fat it has stored under its skin.

Mammals such as dormice, woodchucks, and ground squirrels are *true* hibernators. These mammals sleep all winter in shelters that protect them from the cold. By the time spring arrives, they may weigh only half as much as they did in the fall. Some mammals are so thin when they wake up that they look like toothpicks wearing overcoats. Then, during the summer and fall, they eat a lot and get fat.

This woodchuck looks very thin as it comes out from its long winter sleep.

Winter-Denning

Many people think that bears hibernate, but bears sleep the way we do—only for a longer time. Scientists call this "winter-denning." While a bear is winter-denning, its breathing, heartbeat, and body temperature stay almost normal. Bears can be awakened easily. On warmer days in the winter they often leave their snug dens to prowl around for food.

Raccoons, skunks, and badgers are also part-time winter sleepers. These animals curl up in cozy places to escape the bitter cold. They may sleep for several days or weeks at a time. But on mild winter days they come out for food. You can often find their tracks in the snow.

A Different Winter Sleep

Frogs, snakes, and other "cold-blooded" creatures have hardly any body heat of their own, and no built-in "thermostats." The colder the air gets, the lower their body temperatures drop. If these animals didn't sleep in warm places, they would freeze to death. They drift into another kind of winter sleep. This sleep is called *torpor*.

When the weather gets chilly, some snakes clump together, like a big ball of spaghetti, inside a den. Frogs and many toads burrow into the mud at the bottom of' ponds. Box turtles dig winter homes deep under the ground before it freezes.

Some adult insects, such as moths, grasshoppers, and praying

Some snakes clump together to stay warm and cozy through the winter.

mantises, die before winter comes. But they leave behind "sleeping" offspring in the form of eggs, nymphs, larvae, or pupae. Other adult insects, some kinds of bees, beetles, and butterflies sleep through the cold months. They do not wake up until the air around them gets warm enough.

Hibernating mammals do not wake up until spring. Nevertheless, on February 2, many people wait for the groundhog to come out of its burrow and look for its shadow. But the groundhog, of course, will still be underground, deep in its winter sleep.

 Bookshelf

These books will tell you more about winter sleepers.

Facklam, Margery. *Do Not Disturb: The Mysteries of Animal Hibernation and Sleep.* Boston: Little, Brown, 1989.

Insect Hibernation. Milwaukee, Wisc.: Raintree Publishers, 1986.

Riha, Susanne. *Animals in Winter.* Minneapolis, Minn.: Carolrhoda Books, 1989.

Name _____

Listen to each word. Find the word in the box and circle it.

1.	2.	3.	4.	5.
incline	decide	conflict	reduce	trapeze
inhale	decade	confuse	recent	trooper
include	devote	conclude	recite	turnpike
income	decline	concrete	rickets	trample

6.	7.	8.	9.	10.
adore	tremble	parent	promote	rudder
arise	tribal	parade	partner	rotate
accuse	tribute	pirate	persuade	record
advice	trader	perfume	produce	require

11.	12.	13.	14.	15.
relay	halter	sealing	indent	leather
rely	hailstone	steamer	increase	loaves
relax	haircut	soaking	indeed	labor
repeal	haying	sailing	invite	layer

16.	17.	18.	19.	20.
poacher	headache	floating	detail	mealtime
peanut	hurry	flatboat	disease	meanwhile
peeper	hurray	freezing	deepest	mainly
painter	hungry	failing	dealer	moaning

21.	22.	23.	24.	25.
success	trailer	agree	stormy	airmail
succeed	teammate	abroad	streamer	outside
sunset	thirteen	ahead	streetcar	oatmeal
sweater	treatment	aimless	stairway	eastern

Name _____

 coin    **toy**    **saucer**    **saw**

Circle the word that completes the phrase and write it on the line.

---

1. ball
   boil
   bail

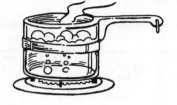

_____ the water

---

6. raid
   ray
   raw

a _____ carrot

---

2. haul
   hail
   heal

_____ the huge logs

---

7. crawl
   crease
   coil

_____ on the rug

---

3. eel
   owl
   oil

an _____ truck

---

8. hear
   hawk
   hike

a large _____

---

4. joy
   jaw
   jay

jump for _____

---

9. shawl
   sauce
   soil

hot fudge _____

---

5. mist
   mean
   moist

a _____ sponge

---

10. boy
    boat
    bawl

a _____ reading

Reading phrases: one-syllable words with **oi, oy, au, aw**

Name _____

Read each riddle. The answers have two words. In each box choose one word from the left column and one word from the right column. Write the two words on the lines below the riddle.

huge	ivy	royal	point
beef	laundry	brave	shortcake
awful	oyster	sharp	parrot
dirty	sausage	ocean	astronaut
raw	dinosaur	strawberry	voyage
poison	cold	noisy	maiden

1. a shellfish that is not cooked

___raw___ ___oyster___

2. clothes that need to be washed

_____ _____

3. a large extinct animal

_____ _____

4. a plant that has clusters of three leaves and causes a rash

_____ _____

5. a bad sore throat and a runny nose

_____ _____

6. a kind of meat

_____ _____

7. a fearless person who travels in space

_____ _____

8. a dessert made from sweet red berries

_____ _____

9. a princess

_____ _____

10. a bird that talks and squawks all the time

_____ _____

11. a trip by boat across the sea

_____ _____

12. the end of a pencil that is not dull

_____ _____

Reading and reasoning: one syllable and more than one syllable words with **oi, oy, au, aw**

Name _____

 tie  field  boot  book

Circle the word that completes the phrase and write it on the line.

1. roots
   reads
   tools

   the _____ of a tree

2. shoot
   sheet
   shield

   King Arthur's _____

3. tied
   took
   tile

   _____ with a ribbon

4. pool
   pie
   peal

   apple _____

5. squeal
   steal
   stool

   sit on a _____

6. brake
   brook
   broil

   a _____ in the forest

7. wait
   weak
   wood

   a pile of _____

8. piece
   pail
   pole

   _____ of the puzzle

9. steam
   school
   scoop

   a big _____ of ice cream

10. choose
    chief
    chain

    the fire _____

Name _____

In two- or three-syllable words, the letters **ie** and **oo** stand for the same sounds as they do in one-syllable words.

cash**ier**   butterfl**ies**   w**oo**dchuck   whirlp**oo**l
cash **ier**   but ter fl**ies**   w**oo**d chuck   whirl p**oo**l

Divide each word below into two syllables. Write each syllable on a line.

relief	_____ _____	bamboo	_____ _____
redwood	_____ _____	believe	_____ _____
cartoon	_____ _____	wooden	_____ _____
candied	_____ _____	toadstools	_____ _____
supplies	_____ _____	rabies	_____ _____

Read each sentence. Choose a word from above that completes the sentence and write it on the line.

1. When Luis said he was six feet tall, I did not _____ him.

2. Mushrooms and _____ look alike to me.

3. The _____ trees are among the oldest and biggest in the United States.

4. Which _____ show on TV do you like best?

5. All the _____ for our camping trip are in our backpacks.

6. Pandas like to eat the leaves of the _____ plant.

7. It was a big _____ to everyone when they found the lost children.

8. We did not think our dog had _____, but we took him to the vet.

9. Mom and I boiled brown sugar and water for the _____ apples.

10. Julie's grandfather has carved more than one hundred _____ animals.

Name _____

 ch**ew**    cl**ou**d    **cow**    cr**ow**

Circle the word that completes the phrase and write it on the line.

1. found
   flea
   flew

   _____ away

2. grew
   greed
   ground

   _____ two inches

3. crawl
   crouch
   crowd

   a large _____

4. meant
   mound
   main

   a _____ of hay

5. mow
   mew
   moo

   _____ the lawn

6. glow
   glove
   goal

   _____ in the dark

7. paint
   prowl
   proud

   _____ parents

8. doom
   dew
   deed

   _____ on the grass

9. plow
   plea
   pound

   a snow _____

10. green
    grow
    growl

    _____ at the thief

Name _____

Read the four headings in each column. Then read the words at the top of the column. Write each word under its correct heading.

sparrow	blouse	outlaw
scout	minnow	trout
trousers	crow	towel
owl	cowboy	flounder

noodles	mouse	mushroom
playground	mew	downstairs
collie	stew	woodchuck
oink	caw	outside

People

_____

_____

_____

Birds

_____

_____

_____

Fish

_____

_____

_____

Things Made of Cloth

_____

_____

_____

Animals

_____

_____

_____

Places

_____

_____

_____

Animal Sounds

_____

_____

_____

Things to Eat

_____

_____

_____

Name _____

k**ey**

Circle the word that completes the phrase and write it on the line.

1. chestnut chimney jockey a brick _____	6. jockey jelly jersey a football _____
2. hockey honey headline _____ stick	7. alley aloud allow a bowling _____
3. battle barley battery a flashlight _____	8. money monkey many my lunch _____
4. daisy donkey kidney stubborn _____	9. pantry parsley pathway a stone _____
5. tower trolley turkey Thanksgiving _____	10. party penny pulley a shiny _____

Name _____

Read each riddle. The answers have two words. In each box choose one word from the left column and one word from the right column. Write the two words on the lines below the riddle.

one	cloud	yellow	jockey
green	thousand	gentle	thief
hot	valley	newborn	crayon
power	afternoon	pretty	rainbow
rain	saw	noon	shower
fried	hamburger	jewel	baby

1. a time in the day when it is very warm

_____ _____

2. a cooked meat

_____ _____

3. the number after 999

_____ _____

4. a dark mass in the sky that will bring a storm

_____ _____

5. a grassy place between two mountains

_____ _____

6. a tool with a motor that is used to cut down trees

_____ _____

7. a child who has just been born

_____ _____

8. a short rain in the middle of the day

_____ _____

9. a robber who steals rings, watches, and gems

_____ _____

10. a kind person who races horses

_____ _____

11. a band of colors in the sky after the rain

_____ _____

12. a stick of wax that is a bright color

_____ _____

Reading and reasoning: one- and two-syllable words with vowel combinations **69**

Name _____

Circle one word that fits BOTH definitions. Write it on the line.
You may use your dictionary.

1. a. a person who is not honest
   b. a long stick with a curved end

   _____

   crook
   croak
   creek

2. a. to take a bath under a spray of water
   b. a short rain

   _____

   shower
   rainbow
   shampoo

3. a. to strike again and again
   b. sixteen ounces

   _____

   fasten
   pound
   2 cupsful

4. a. a noble person
   b. to number things one by one

   _____

   count
   queen
   point

5. a. a game played by two teams on a
      long field
   b. an oval-shaped ball

   _____

   hockey
   basketball
   football

6. a. a place where you wash and dry
      clothes
   b. dirty clothes

   _____

   laundry
   bathtub
   sweater

7. a. to pass through the mouth and throat
   b. a bird with a forked tail

   _____

   swallow
   crow
   eaten

8. a. the opening that we use for eating
   b. the place where a river enters the
      ocean

   _____

   teeth
   mouth
   stream

9. a. a dark space in the shape of a person
      or thing
   b. to follow someone closely

   _____

   sound
   shadow
   look

Name _____

Read the story. Circle the words to complete the sentences.
Write the words in the sentences.

1.	When Tom Atkeson was a boy, his father would bring home things for them to look at together. They enjoyed shells, rocks, animals, and other things from the _____.	outdoors cartoon shadow
2.	Later, Tom studied forestry at college. Then he went to work at a place where birds and animals would be protected—a _____ refuge.	rowboat housework wildlife
3.	Tom's first job was to study the land and make a map of the new refuge. He also had to mark the _____ lines around the 20 miles of the refuge.	rooftop boundary downstairs
4.	This was a good time to decide where to plant trees and _____. Tom wanted to provide food that would attract wild creatures to the refuge.	drawings cowards berries
5.	When World War II began, Tom Atkeson left to join the Army. A land mine exploded and _____ his hands and arms, part of his face, and one kneecap.	royal destroyed trooper
6.	Tom spent months in the hospital. He was blind, he was lame, and he had hooks for hands. But he _____ he could go back to the outdoor work he loved.	borrowed believed bounced
7.	Tom was _____ when he was hired to work at the refuge again. From memory, he still knew the land, probably better than anyone who could see.	crowded wooden overjoyed

© The Continental Press, Inc.

Reading a story and expressive writing **71**

8. At first Tom worked _____, in the office. Soon he worked on the refuge and became manager. He knew all about the refuge and the animals that lived there.	indoors mildew outlaw
9. Forty different kinds of mammals live at the refuge—otters, beavers, deer, _____, and others. Tom's hard work also attracted many types of birds.	voices clowns raccoons
10. Tom Atkeson hates the word "handicapped." The only special help he _____ is the light touch of a person at his elbow to guide him.	allows avoids annoys
11. The Wheeler Wildlife Refuge is a fantastic place. Tom Atkeson's wonderful outlook and his _____ work have made it so.	thousand outstanding spoonful

Write a story about a person you admire who overcame a problem.

_____

_____

_____

_____

_____

_____

_____

_____

TALES

FROM AROUND THE WORLD

The Monkey and the Crocodile

A monkey lived in a great tree on a riverbank. In the river there were many crocodiles.

A crocodile watched the monkeys for a long time, and one day she said to her son, "My son, get one of those monkeys for me. I want the heart of a monkey to eat."

"How am I to catch a monkey?" asked the little crocodile. "I do not travel on land, and the monkey does not go into the water."

"Put your wits to work, and you'll find a way," said the mother. And the little crocodile thought and thought.

"How queer!" said the stupid crocodile. "Do you mean to say that you left your heart back there in the tree?"

"That is what I mean," said the monkey. "If you want my heart, we must go back to the tree and get it. But we are so near the island where the ripe fruit is, please take me there first."

"No, monkey," said the crocodile, "I'll take you straight back to your tree. Never mind the ripe fruit. Get your heart and bring it to me at once. Then we'll see about going to the island."

"Very well," said the monkey.

But no sooner had the monkey jumped onto the bank of the river than—wisk! he ran into the tree.

From the topmost branches he called down to the crocodile in the water below. "My heart is way up here! If you want it, come for it, come for it!"

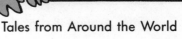

At last he said to himself, "I know what I'll do. I'll get that monkey that lives in a big tree on the riverbank. He wishes to go across the river to the island where the fruit is so ripe."

So the crocodile swam to the tree where the monkey lived.

"Oh, monkey," he called, "come with me over to the island where the fruit is so ripe."

"How can I go with you?" asked the monkey. "I do not swim."

"No—but I do. I will take you over on my back," said the crocodile.

The monkey was greedy and wanted the ripe fruit, so he jumped down on the crocodile's back.

"Off we go!" said the crocodile.

"This is a fine ride you are giving me!" said the monkey.

"Do you think so? Well, how do you like this?" asked the crocodile, diving under the water.

"Oh, don't!" cried the monkey, as he went under the water. He was afraid to let go, and he did not know what to do under the water.

When the crocodile came up, the monkey sputtered and choked. "Why did you take me under water, crocodile?" he asked.

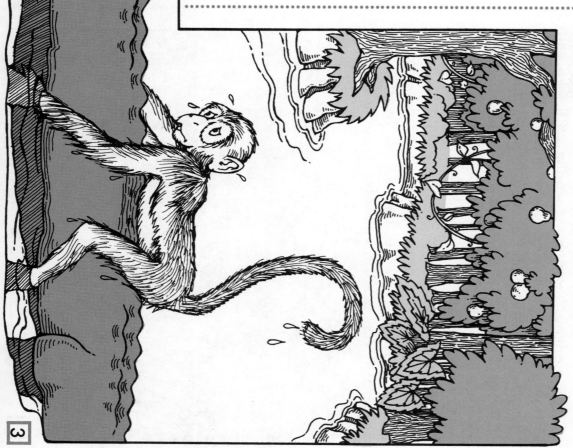

"I am going to kill you by keeping you under water," answered the crocodile. "My mother wants monkey heart to eat, and I'm going to take yours to her."

"I wish you had told me you wanted my heart," said the monkey. "Then I might have brought it with me."

3

Name _____

Listen to each word. Find the word in the box and circle it.

1.	2.	3.	4.	5.
belling	awning	autumn	porridge	maroon
boiling	anyone	onion	drawbridge	mowers
bailing	annoy	outer	drowning	marvel
bolting	await	attend	draining	married

6.	7.	8.	9.	10.
underneath	curfew	disagree	cardboard	volley
underside	curtain	discontent	coward	volume
understand	kerchief	discount	cleared	volcano
understood	corkscrew	display	coastland	voyage

11.	12.	13.	14.	15.
dogwood	brewing	mellow	movies	sounding
doghouse	border	minnow	mowers	southeast
dogsled	borrow	midday	moisten	soybean
dugout	broiled	mildew	mouthful	saucepan

16.	17.	18.	19.	20.
oiler	afraid	hauling	rusty	without
owner	avoid	hello	roundup	window
outdoor	award	holler	rooster	wisdom
author	arrow	hollow	rustler	worries

21.	22.	23.	24.	25.
shrewd	surround	drier	howdy	village
shallow	severe	dreamer	honey	vault
shampoo	sewer	drowning	haunted	vowel
shadow	surface	drawer	howling	vanilla

Action words, called verbs, can have the endings **s**, **es**, **ed**, and **ing**.
These endings tell us when the action takes place.

If a one-syllable word ends in a single consonant after a short vowel, double the consonant before you add **ed** or **ing**.	If a word ends in **e**, drop the **e** before you add **ed** or **ing**.	If a word ends in **y** after a consonant, change the **y** to **i** before you add **es** or **ed**.
grip + **ed** = gripped grip + **ing** = gripping	race + **ed** = raced race + **ing** = racing	cry + **es** = cries cry + **ed** = cried
Do not double the consonant when you add **s** or **es**. grip + **s** = grips	Do not drop the **e** when you add **s**. race + **s** = races	Do not change **y** to **i** when you add **ing**. cry + **ing** = crying

Read the words below. Add the ending to each word and write the new word on the line.

empty + ed _____   pity + ed _____

teach + es _____   hide + ing _____

explore + s _____   trap + ed _____

try + ing _____   fly + es _____

Choose the correct word to complete each sentence. Write it in the sentence.

1. Every day Bruce _____ his backyard for interesting insects.

2. He is watching a caterpillar that is _____ in the rosebush.

3. "How long before it will be a butterfly that _____ from one bush to another?" he asks.

4. Yesterday he saw something very interesting as he _____ the birdbath and filled it again.

5. He saw a spider that had _____ a dragonfly twice its size.

6. Bruce _____ the dragonfly, but he knew the spider must not go hungry.

7. Bruce likes to read books about insects, and he also _____ his little sister about them.

8. He is _____ to learn the correct names of all the insects he sees in his yard.

Name _____

The endings **er** and **est** are added to base words to compare things or actions. We use **er** to compare two things. We use **est** to compare more than two things.

If a word ends in a single consonant after a short vowel, double the consonant before you add **er** or **est**.	If a word ends in **e**, drop the **e** before you add **er** or **est**.	If a word ends in **y** after a consonant, change the **y** to **i** before you add **er** or **est**.
thin + **er** = thinner thin + **est** = thinnest	cute + **er** = cuter cute + **est** = cutest	lucky + **er** = luckier lucky + **est** = luckiest

Read each sentence. Add **er** or **est** to the base word to complete each sentence. Write the word in the sentence.

1. The sun, which is a star, and nine planets make up most of our solar system. The sun is the _____ star to Earth and the other planets.

2. The diameter of the sun is 865,000 miles. It is much_____ than any planet.

3. Jupiter and Saturn are huge. Mercury, Mars, and Pluto are very small. Mercury is the _____ planet of all.

4. Saturn has many rings around it. Some people think it is a _____ planet than Venus.

5. The planet Mercury has extreme temperatures. It is one of the coldest and also one of the _____ planets.

6. Venus is the planet _____ to Earth. It is 26 million miles away.

close

large

small

pretty

hot

near

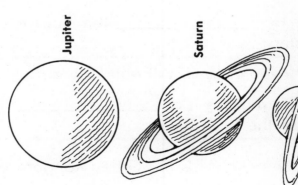

Name _____

Choose the correct word to complete each sentence.
Circle the word and write it in the sentence.

1. In the book *The Beast in Ms. Rooney's Room*, Richard _____ about many things from Mrs. Paris, the reading teacher.	learner learns learning
2. In *Beezus and Romona*, Beezus has many problems, but Romona is her _____ problem.	bigger begins biggest
3. In *Cam Jensen and the Mystery at the Monkey House*, Cam and her friends _____ the mystery of the missing monkeys.	solves solved solving
4. In *Pippi Longstocking*, Pippi's tall tales of things that happened to her are _____ than you expect them to be.	strange stranger strangest
5. In the *Chalk Box Kid*, a lonely boy spends much of his time _____ pictures.	draws drawing draw
6. In *Charlotte's Web*, Wilbur, the pig, is _____ by a rat and a spider.	saves saving saved
7. In *Miss Nelson Is Missing*, the students find out that Miss Swamp can be much _____ than Miss Nelson.	cranky crankier crankiest
8. In *The Case of the Nervous Newsboy*, McGurk looked hard at everything. He _____ the clues to help him solve the mystery.	studying study studied
9. In *How to Eat Fried Worms*, Bill eats a worm every day for 15 days. First he mashes it or _____ it in some way to disguise the taste.	fixing feeds fixes
10. In *The One in the Middle Is the Green Kangaroo*, Freddy _____ and jumped better than the other children.	hopped hoped hopping

78   Reading sentences: inflectional endings **s, es, ed, ing** and comparatives

Name _____

The word **plural** means "more than one."

To make many words plural, add **s**.	If a word ends in a consonant plus **y**, change the **y** to **i** and add **es**.	If a word ends in **f** or **fe**, change the **f** or **fe** to **v** and add **es**.
tadpole**s** muffin**s**	pony poni**es**	thief thie**ves**
If a word ends in **sh**, **ch**, **tch**, **s**, **ss**, or **x**, add **es**.	If a word ends in a vowel plus **y**, simply add **s**.	If a word ends in **ff**, simply add **s**.
match**es** bus**es** box**es**	weekday**s**	cuff**s**

Read the words below. Say the plural of the word and write it.

wife _____   wristwatch _____

harpoon _____   chimney _____

cavity _____   sheriff _____

elf _____   sandwich _____

Read the sentences below. Choose the singular or plural of any word above that completes the sentence. Write the correct word on the line.

1. Justin needed his _____ to tell when it was time to go home.

2. When I came home from the dentist, I said, "Look, Mom,

   no _____."

3. The men, their _____, and their children were all invited to the family picnic.

4. Tessa wanted to make two ham and cheese _____.

5. The Eskimos use _____ for hunting whales for food.

6. The _____ showed his badge to the crowd of people on the street.

7. Each house has a brick fireplace with a big _____.

8. Do you know a story about a shoemaker and some _____ that helped him?

Plurals: **s**, **es**, **y** to **ies**, **f** to **ves**

Name _____

Read each riddle. The answers have two words. In each box choose one word from the left column and one word from the right column. Write the two words on the line below the riddle.

brownest	monkeys	dirty	scarves
flowering	stories	dancing	handcuffs
circus	calves	warm	poppies
largest	bushes	silver	couches
funniest	loaves	prettiest	knives
frisky	berries	harder	ladies

1. baby cows that are lively and playful

_____ _____

2. tales about people and animals who perform in a big tent

_____ _____

3. bread that is darker than the others

_____ _____

4. shrubs that are in blossom

_____ _____

5. the animals in the zoo that made us laugh the hardest

_____ _____

6. the biggest fruit on the bushes

_____ _____

7. women who are moving in time to music

_____ _____

8. what people wear around their necks in winter

_____ _____

9. tools for cutting that are not clean

_____ _____

10. sofas that are more firm than some others

_____ _____

11. a pair of metal rings to lock around someone's wrists

_____ _____

12. red flowers that are the most beautiful

_____ _____

Name _____

Use the words in the box to fill in the blanks and discover the code. Each letter of the alphabet has a number code. Find the correct letter for each number. For instance, the number **5** is always used for the letter **i** and **22** is used for **m**. As you go along, fill in the letters in the code box to help you.

leaves	shiniest	thinner	axes
quizzing	hobbies	copied	grumbling

1. a word that means muttering
   unhappily

   — — — — — — — — —
   1 6 13 22 18 15 5 9 1

2. a word that means the brightest

   — — — — — — — —
   8 11 5 9 5 2 8 10

3. slimmer

   — — — — — — —
   10 11 5 9 9 2 6

4. made another one that is just
   the same

   — — — — — —
   25 3 20 5 2 16

5. asking questions

   — — — — — — — —
   14 13 5 12 12 5 9 1

6. green flat parts of plants that
   grow from the stems

   — — — — — —
   15 2 4 19 2 8

7. things you like to do in your
   spare time

   — — — — — — —
   11 3 18 18 5 2 8

8. tools used to cut down small
   trees

   — — — —
   4 21 2 8

```
                    THE CODE BOX
                         w
—   —   —   —   —   —   —   —   —   —   —   —   —
1   2   3   4   5   6   7   8   9   10  11  12  13
            j                       y   k       f
—   —   —   —   —   —   —   —   —   —   —   —   —
14  15  16  17  18  19  20  21  22  23  24  25  26
```

Now use the code to answer the following riddle:
When can three big people go out under one umbrella and not get wet?

— — — —   — —   — —   — — —   — — — — — —
7 11 2 9   5 10   5 8   9 3 10   6 4 5 9 5 9 1

Puzzle page: inflectional endings   **81**

Stopping by Woods
on a Snowy Evening

Whose woods these are I think I know.
His house is in the village though;
He will not see me stopping here
To watch his woods fill up with snow.

My little horse must think it queer
To stop without a farmhouse near
Between the woods and frozen lake
The darkest evening of the year.

He gives his harness bells a shake
To ask if there is some mistake.
The only other sound's the sweep
Of easy wind and downy flake.

The woods are lovely, dark and deep.
But I have promises to keep,
And miles to go before I sleep,
And miles to go before I sleep.

Robert Frost

Name _____

Read the story. Circle the words to complete the sentences.
Write the words in the sentences.

1. Five wolf pups are born in a den dug into the side of a hill. These _____ have woolly hair and floppy ears, and they are blind.	numbers babies bottles
2. When they are twelve days old, the baby _____ open their blue eyes. Later, their eyes will change to a yellow color.	flowers fishes wolves
3. When they are about three weeks old, the pups come out of the den and play. They enjoy rolling about and _____ each other with their noses.	nuzzling sparkling whistling
4. Sometimes pups fight with each other. Finally one gives up and rolls over on its back. Then the _____ wolf stands over the loser and raises its tail.	dimmest fluffier stronger
5. In this way each wolf learns its place, or rank, in the wolf pack. At six months of age, the pups start to hunt for _____ .	himself themselves yourselves
6. Each wolf keeps its rank in the wolf pack. As they grow older, the wolves do not fight because their sharp teeth would _____ each other.	hurt hurts hurting
7. The _____ and strongest wolf in the pack is like a king or leader. But all the wolves in a pack work together as a team when they hunt.	laziest lamest largest

Reading a story and expressive writing

8. They also work together _____ the newborn pups. They find food for the pups and protect them.	richest richer raising
9. A wolf uses its fine sense of smell in _____ animals. Wolves travel many miles to find food. Deer, moose, and other animals are often hunted.	trapped trappers tracking
10. The moose knows how to defend itself. Its hard _____ can crack a wolf's bones. But still the wolves like to hunt these larger animals.	hooves halves huffs
11. During a hunt, a wolf often _____, and then the pack knows where it is. Sometimes wolf families howl together just for the fun of it.	huskies howls hounds

Pretend you are a wolf and tell
what it is like to hunt for a moose.

_____

_____

_____

_____

_____

_____

_____

The Wolfman David Mech

Dr. Mech will study this wolf and then set it free.

Out of the forest walks The Wolfman. Across his shoulders he carries an animal. Is this wolfman the movie monster who comes out when the moon is full? Far from it! This is a real-life scientist named David Mech. (His name rhymes with "peach.") He is carrying a tranquilized wolf he has captured in order to study it. Dr. Mech probably knows more about wolves than anyone else. That's why some people call him "The Wolfman."

"I guess I was always interested in wolves," says Dr. Mech. "In college, I decided to study wolves. Nobody knew much about them back then. I hiked through the woods, looking for the wolves. I walked over 1,500 miles—and I saw only three wolves. I decided there had to be a better way!" And he found one.

Tracking Wolves

A few scientists were just starting to track animals from airplanes. Dr. Mech came up with a sturdy leather collar that could be clamped around a wolf's neck. Built into each collar was a very small radio transmitter. Each battery-operated collar transmitted, or sent out, beeps.

Dr. Mech can fly around overhead and tune in his radio receiver. With his radio on, he can pick up the beeps of whatever wolf is around.

In a plane Dr. Mech picks up beeps from the radio transmitter in the wolf's collar.

Using his radio-tracking method, Dr. Mech learned a lot about wolves. He found that wolves hunt only for food. And they often go hungry. They hunt mostly for deer or moose in packs of two to eight wolves. "They may go as long as two weeks between meals," says Dr. Mech.

Dogs and Wolves

"Dogs and wolves are very closely related," the scientist explains. "Members of a wolf pack act toward each other much as your pet dog acts toward you. For instance, when two pack members have been apart for a while, they rush together, licking each other's faces and wagging their tails like crazy. It's just the way your dog might act when you come home from school!"

But if wolves are so much like dogs, why are so many people afraid of them?

These wolves are excited as they greet each other after being apart.

"Partly because of all those fairy tales we read," says Dr. Mech. In *The Three Little Pigs* and *Little Red Riding Hood*, the wolf is always the bad guy.

But wolves don't huff and puff and blow houses down. And wolves wouldn't gobble you up.

"There has not been one single case of a healthy wolf attacking a human in North America!" Dr. Mech says firmly. "I've been right out there in the forests with them—for about 25 years. And I've never felt I was in even the slightest danger!"

A Threat to the Wolves

Wolves need wild places to live. Dr. Mech is worried that these areas will disappear. Then wolves may become extinct. He is working to save their habitat, the places where they live. And he plans to keep on studying wolves, too. The more that people know about wolves, the more they will understand that there is no such thing as a big bad wolf.

 Bookshelf

These books will tell you more about wolves.

Fox, Dr. Michael. *The Wolf.* New York: Coward, McCann, & Geoghegan, 1973.

Hogan, Paula Z. *The Wolf.* Milwaukee, Wisc.: Raintree, 1979.

Lawrence, R. D. *Wolves.* Boston: Little, Brown, 1990.

Name _____

Listen to each word. Find the word in the box and circle it.

1.	2.	3.	4.	5.
scoops	squash	plans	scrapping	hires
scooped	squashed	planed	scraping	hurries
scooper	squashing	planned	scraped	hurried
scooping	squashes	planes	scrapped	hurrying

6.	7.	8.	9.	10.
filling	destroys	hatched	study	caning
filled	dirties	hatchet	studied	cans
filed	dirtied	hatching	studies	canning
filing	destroyed	hatches	studying	canes

11.	12.	13.	14.	15.
thief	carried	chairs	halves	taxes
thicken	carrying	cheers	have	tracks
threats	caring	cherries	half	tacks
thieves	carries	churches	haven't	ticks

16.	17.	18.	19.	20.
sillier	wetting	sharpest	braves	hundreds
silver	western	sharpen	bravest	hungriest
silliest	wetter	sharper	bravely	hungrier
silkier	wets	sharing	braver	hunger

21.	22.	23.	24.	25.
thickest	saddest	happen	slime	rips
thicken	saddles	happiness	slimmer	ripper
thicker	sadder	happiest	slimmest	riper
thicket	sadden	happier	slipper	ripest

Name _____

A **dictionary** is a book of words listed in alphabetical order.
It gives the spelling and meaning of each word and tells how to pronounce each word.

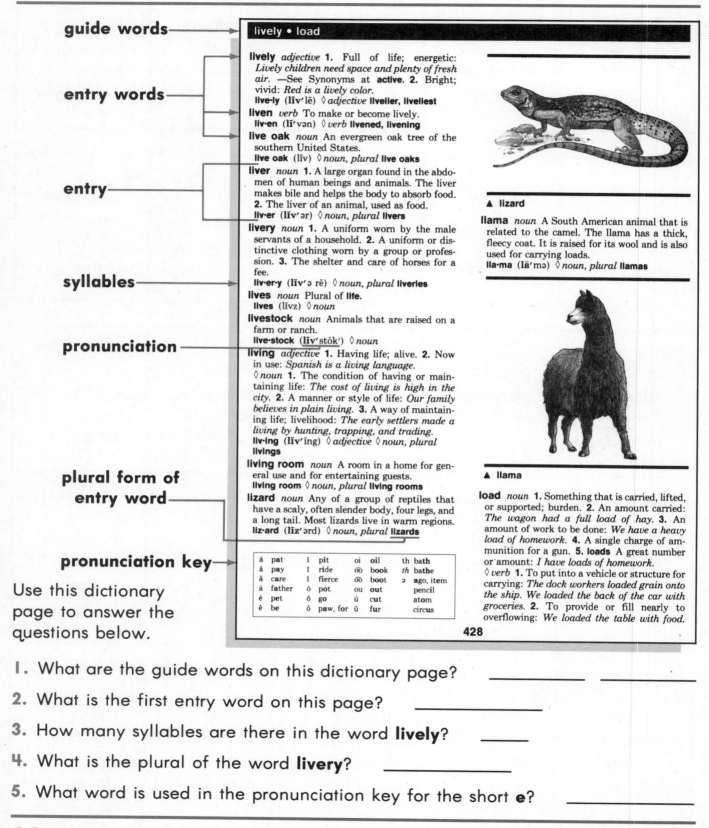

guide words ⟶
entry words ⟶
entry ⟶
syllables ⟶
pronunciation ⟶
plural form of entry word ⟶
pronunciation key ⟶

lively • load

lively *adjective* **1.** Full of life; energetic: *Lively children need space and plenty of fresh air.* —See Synonyms at **active. 2.** Bright; vivid: *Red is a lively color.*
live·ly (līv′lē) ◊ *adjective* **livelier, liveliest**

liven *verb* To make or become lively.
liv·en (lī′vən) ◊ *verb* **livened, livening**

live oak *noun* An evergreen oak tree of the southern United States.
live oak (līv) ◊ *noun, plural* **live oaks**

liver *noun* **1.** A large organ found in the abdomen of human beings and animals. The liver makes bile and helps the body to absorb food. **2.** The liver of an animal, used as food.
liv·er (līv′ər) ◊ *noun, plural* **livers**

livery *noun* **1.** A uniform worn by the male servants of a household. **2.** A uniform or distinctive clothing worn by a group or profession. **3.** The shelter and care of horses for a fee.
liv·er·y (līv′ə rē) ◊ *noun, plural* **liveries**

lives *noun* Plural of **life.**
lives (līvz) ◊ *noun*

livestock *noun* Animals that are raised on a farm or ranch.
live·stock (līv′stŏk′) ◊ *noun*

living *adjective* **1.** Having life; alive. **2.** Now in use: *Spanish is a living language.* ◊ *noun* **1.** The condition of having or maintaining life: *The cost of living is high in the city.* **2.** A manner or style of life: *Our family believes in plain living.* **3.** A way of maintaining life; livelihood: *The early settlers made a living by hunting, trapping, and trading.*
liv·ing (līv′ĭng) ◊ *adjective* ◊ *noun, plural* **livings**

living room *noun* A room in a home for general use and for entertaining guests.
living room ◊ *noun, plural* **living rooms**

lizard *noun* Any of a group of reptiles that have a scaly, often slender body, four legs, and a long tail. Most lizards live in warm regions.
liz·ard (lĭz′ərd) ◊ *noun, plural* **lizards**

▲ **lizard**

llama *noun* A South American animal that is related to the camel. The llama has a thick, fleecy coat. It is raised for its wool and is also used for carrying loads.
lla·ma (lä′mə) ◊ *noun, plural* **llamas**

▲ **llama**

load *noun* **1.** Something that is carried, lifted, or supported; burden. **2.** An amount carried: *The wagon had a full load of hay.* **3.** An amount of work to be done: *We have a heavy load of homework.* **4.** A single charge of ammunition for a gun. **5. loads** A great number or amount: *I have loads of homework.* ◊ *verb* **1.** To put into a vehicle or structure for carrying: *The dock workers loaded grain onto the ship. We loaded the back of the car with groceries.* **2.** To provide or fill nearly to overflowing: *We loaded the table with food.*

â	pat	ĭ	pit	oi	oil	th	bath
ā	pay	ī	ride	oo	book	th	bathe
â	care	î	fierce	oo	boot	ə	ago, item
ä	father	ŏ	pot	ou	out		pencil
ĕ	pet	ō	go	ŭ	cut		atom
ē	be	ô	paw, for	û	fur		circus

428

Use this dictionary page to answer the questions below.

1. What are the guide words on this dictionary page? _____ _____

2. What is the first entry word on this page? _____

3. How many syllables are there in the word **lively**? _____

4. What is the plural of the word **livery**? _____

5. What word is used in the pronunciation key for the short **e**? _____

88 Introduction to the dictionary

Name _____

The word **lizard** is an **entry word**.
Everything a dictionary tells you about it is an **entry**.

> **lizard** *noun* Any of a group of reptiles that
> have a scaly, often slender body, four legs, and
> a long tail. Most lizards live in warm regions.
> **liz·ard** (lĭz′ ərd) ◊ *noun, plural* **lizards**

The entry words in a dictionary are listed in alphabetical order.

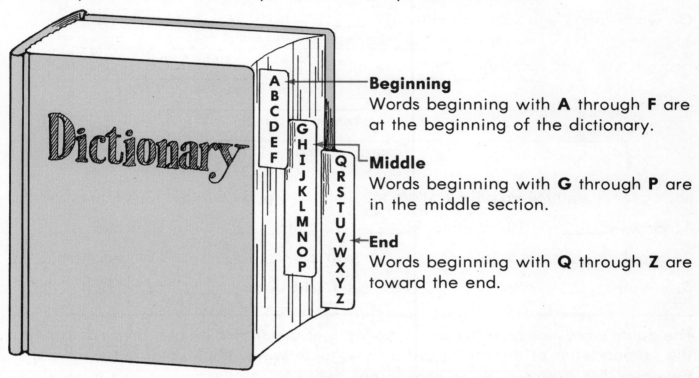

Beginning
Words beginning with **A** through **F** are
at the beginning of the dictionary.

Middle
Words beginning with **G** through **P** are
in the middle section.

End
Words beginning with **Q** through **Z** are
toward the end.

In what section of a dictionary will you find each of these entry words?
Write **B** for Beginning, **M** for Middle, or **E** for End.

1. fox	_____	9. nuthatch	_____	17. horse	_____
2. ostrich	_____	10. antelope	_____	18. quail	_____
3. iguana	_____	11. walrus	_____	19. deer	_____
4. yak	_____	12. leopard	_____	20. panther	_____
5. cheetah	_____	13. buzzard	_____	21. jackal	_____
6. monkey	_____	14. rooster	_____	22. zebra	_____
7. squirrel	_____	15. tiger	_____	23. vulture	_____
8. gorilla	_____	16. elephant	_____	24. kangaroo	_____

Name _____

Guide words are the words found at the top of each dictionary page.
Guide words are the first and last entry words on the page.
All the entry words are listed in alphabetical order.

The guide words at the top of four dictionary pages are shown below.
To find the word **citizen** in the dictionary,
  • look first for guide words that begin with **c**, the first letter in **citizen**
  • look next for guide words that begin with **ci**, the first two letters in **citizen**

On which page will you find **citizen**? _____

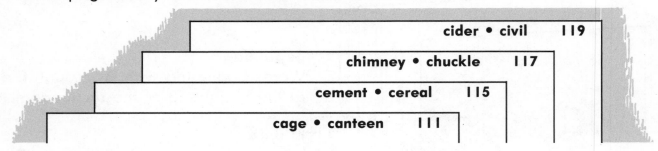

cider • civil   119
chimney • chuckle   117
cement • cereal   115
cage • canteen   111

Look at each entry word below. Write the dictionary page number it will be found on.

1. circus _____   4. chipmunk _____   7. calf _____   10. cake _____

2. canal _____   5. center _____   8. cent _____   11. chopstick _____

3. cinder _____   6. city _____   9. chowder _____   12. cereal _____

The guide words for four more dictionary pages are shown below. If you do not find the second letter of an entry word in any guide word, think what letters it comes between. For example, **se** in **seal** comes between **sc** in **scoop** and **sh** in **shell**.

On which page will you find **seal**? _____

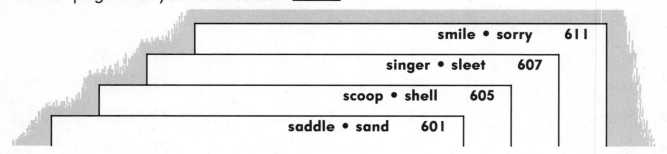

smile • sorry   611
singer • sleet   607
scoop • shell   605
saddle • sand   601

Look at each entry word below. Write the dictionary page number it will be found on.

1. smoke _____   4. shake _____   7. score _____   10. sled _____

2. seven _____   5. salad _____   8. snow _____   11. snail _____

3. song _____   6. skunk _____   9. sister _____   12. sky _____

Name _____

Guide words at the top of each dictionary page are the first and last entry words on that page. All the entry words are listed in alphabetical order.

To find the word **mammal** in the dictionary,
- look first for guide words that begin with the first letter of **mammal**
- then look for guide words that begin with the first and second letters in **mammal**
- then look for guide words that begin with the first three letters in **mammal**

On which page below will you find **mammal**? _____ **major**? _____ **maid**? _____

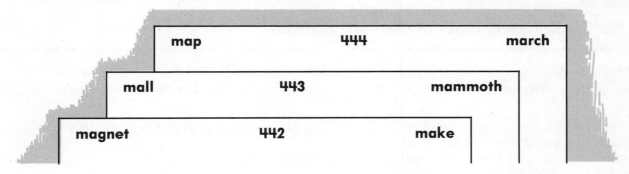

map	444	march
mall	443	mammoth
magnet	442	make

The guide words for four dictionary pages are shown below.

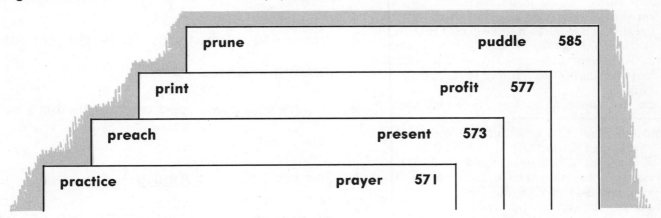

prune	puddle	585
print	profit	577
preach	present	573
practice	prayer	571

Look at each entry word below and decide which dictionary page it is on. Write the correct page number after each word.

> **Remember:** Entry words are listed in alphabetical order.

1. predict _____
2. prance _____
3. prison _____
4. problem _____

5. pry _____
6. prank _____
7. public _____
8. prepare _____

9. prefer _____
10. product _____
11. prune _____
12. prairie _____

Guide words and alphabetical sequence to the third letter

Name _____

An **entry** in a dictionary gives the spelling, pronunciation, and meaning of the entry word. Different dictionaries may give this information in a different order. Here are entries from two dictionaries for the word **huddle**. Compare them.

entry word
────── part of speech

huddle *noun* A closely packed group or crowd: *There was a huddle around the warmth of the campfire.*
◊ *verb* To crowd close or put close together.
hud·dle (hŭd′l) ◊ *noun, plural* **huddles**
◊ *verb* **huddled, huddling**

entry word
part of speech

¹hud·dle \'həd-l\ *vb* **hud·dled; hud·dling**
1 : to crowd, push, or pile together ⟨people *huddled* in a doorway⟩ **2** : CONFER **3** : to curl up ⟨*huddled* by the fire⟩
²huddle *n* **1** : a closely packed group **2** : MEETING, CONFERENCE

pronunciation ─┘

There are several **meanings** for the verb **huddle**.

───────────────────────────────────

Read each dictionary entry on the left. Then read each sentence and write the number of the correct meaning from the dictionary entry for the underlined word.

canteen *noun* **1.** A container for carrying liquid, as drinking water. **2.** A store, as in a factory or on a military base, where supplies and refreshments are sold or provided.
can·teen (kăn tēn′) ◊ *noun, plural* **canteens**

ice *noun* **1.** Water that has been frozen solid. **2.** A frozen dessert made of crushed ice flavored with sweet fruit juice or syrup.
◊ *verb* **1.** To make cold or keep cold with ice: *We iced the bottles of juice for the picnic.* **2.** To become covered with ice: *The streets iced over during the freezing rain.* **3.** To put icing on.
ice (īs) ◊ *noun, plural* **ices** ◊ *verb* **iced, icing**

mouse *noun* **1.** A small furry animal with a thin, almost hairless tail. Some kinds live in or near houses of human beings. **2.** A small device on some computers that is held in the hand and used to move the cursor.
mouse (mous) ◊ *noun, plural* **mice**

nose *noun* **1.** The part of the human face or an animal's head that contains the nostrils and organs of smell. **2.** The sense of smell: *The dog's nose told it that food was being cooked.* **3.** Something, as the forward end of an airplane, rocket, or submarine that looks somewhat like a nose.
◊ *verb* **1.** To perceive by or as if by smell: *The dog nosed out the scent of the fox.* **2.** To touch, push, or examine with the nose; nuzzle. **3.** To pry into other people's business. **4.** To move forward cautiously: *The barge nosed past the dock.*
nose (nōz) ◊ *noun, plural* **noses** ◊ *verb* **nosed, nosing**

1. We will buy some hot food at the canteen. _____

2. Fill your canteen with water before the hike. _____

3. Please ice my birthday cake with chocolate frosting. _____ (verb)

4. The trees stayed iced over until the sun came out. _____

5. Our cat caught a mouse. _____

6. Ann knows how to use a mouse to move words around on the computer. _____

7. The plane nosed into the narrow hangar. _____ (verb)

8. A raccoon can nose out ripe corn in the dark. _____ (verb)

FULL PRONUNCIATION KEY

The dictionary tells us the pronunciation of each entry word, or how to say it. Usually there is a **Full Pronunciation Key** at the front of the dictionary. The key shows the letters or symbols used for each sound. Notice that there are several sounds for each of the vowels.

Sounds	Sample Words
ă	as in rat, laugh
ā	ape, aid, pay
â	air, care, wear
ä	father, koala, yard
b	bib, cabbage
ch	church, stitch
d	deed, mailed, puddle
ě	pet, pleasure, any
ē	be, bee, easy, piano
f	fast, fife, off, phrase, rough
g	gag, get, finger
h	hat, who
hw	which, where
ĭ	if, pit, busy
ī	by, pie, high
î	dear, deer, fierce, mere
j	judge, gem
k	cat, kick, school
kw	choir, quick
l	lid, needle, tall
m	am, man, dumb
n	no, sudden
ng	thing, ink
ŏ	horrible, pot
ō	go, row, toe, though
ô	all, caught, for, paw
oi	boy, noise, oil

Sounds	Sample Words
ou	as in cow, out
o͝o	full, took, wolf
o͞o	boot, fruit, flew
p	pop, happy
r	roar, rhyme
s	miss, sauce, scene, see
sh	dish, ship, sugar, tissue
t	tight, stopped
th	bath, thin
th	bathe, this
ŭ	cut, flood, rough, some
û	circle, fur, heard, term, turn, urge, word
v	cave, valve, vine
w	with, wolf
y	yes, yolk, onion
yo͝o	cure
yo͞o	abuse, use
z	rose, size, xylophone, zebra
zh	garage, pleasure, vision
ə	about, silent, pencil, lemon, circus

Stress
Shown by accent marks ′ and ′ and by heavy, dark letters.
dic·tion·ar·y (dĭk′shə nĕr′ē)

The symbols for the vowel sounds are so important that they are shown again, usually on every other page, in a **Short Pronunciation Key**.

SHORT PRONUNCIATION KEY

ă	pat	ĭ	pit	oi	oil	th	bath
ā	pay	ī	ride	o͝o	book	th	bathe
â	care	î	fierce	o͞o	boot	ə	ago, item
ä	father	ŏ	pot	ou	out		pencil
ě	pet	ō	go	ŭ	cut		atom
ē	be	ô	paw, for	û	fur		circus

Look at each entry word below and its pronunciation. Then circle the word that rhymes with one of the syllables. If you need help, use the pronunciation key.

1. volcano (vŏl **kā**′nō)   The second syllable rhymes with: **may**   **my**   **me**

2. hurricane (**hûr**′ĭ kān′)   The last syllable rhymes with: **man**   **main**   **mean**

3. hemisphere (**hěm**′ĭ sfîr)   The last syllable rhymes with: **her**   **hire**   **hear**

4. agriculture (**ăg**′rĭ kŭl′chər)   The first syllable rhymes with: **rage**   **rag**   **rig**

5. accurate (**ăk**′yər ĭt)   The last syllable rhymes with: **mate**   **met**   **mitt**

Name _____

Read the entry for each word below.
These are words you might find in your science book.

atmosphere *noun* **1.** The gas that surrounds a body in space, especially the air that surrounds the earth. **2.** The air or climate of a place: *The desert has a dry atmosphere.* **3.** The general environment in a place: *We like the busy atmosphere of the classroom.* **at·mos·phere** (ăt′mə sfîr′) ◊ *noun, plural* **atmospheres**

chlorophyll *noun* A green pigment composed of carbon, hydrogen, magnesium, nitrogen, and oxygen, found in green plants and other living things. **chlo·ro·phyll** (klôr′ə fĭl) ◊ *noun*

bacteria *plural noun* Tiny one-celled organisms. Some bacteria help digest food; other bacteria cause diseases. **bac·te·ri·a** (băk tîr′ē ə) ◊ *plural noun*

erosion *noun* The process of being worn away bit by bit, as by water or wind. **e·ro·sion** (ĭ rō′zhən) ◊ *noun*

camouflage *noun* The disguising of people, animals, or things, especially in order to make them look like what is around them. ◊ *verb* To hide or disguise by camouflage. **cam·ou·flage** (kăm′ə fläzh′) ◊ *noun* ◊ *verb* **camouflaged, camouflaging**

pollute *verb* To make dirty or impure; contaminate: *Gasoline exhaust pollutes the air.* **pol·lute** (pə lo͞ot′) ◊ *verb* **polluted, polluting**

Look at the pronunciation of each entry word above. Circle the correct answer to complete each sentence and write it on the line. If you need help, look back at the pronunciation key on page 93.

1. In the word **erosion**, the letter **e** stands for the same sound as _____.

the **e** in **leg**
the **i** in **hit**
the **u** in **cut**

2. In the word **atmosphere**, the letters **ph** stand for the same sound as _____.

the **f** in **fun**
the **p** in **pet**
the **th** in **thank**

3. In the word **camouflage**, the letters **ou** stand for the same sound as _____.

the **ow** in **cow**
the **e** in **pet**
the **a** in **about**

4. In the word **bacteria**, the letter **i** stands for the same sound as _____.

the **i** in **hike**
the **ee** in **meet**
the **ai** in **paid**

5. In the word **pollute**, the letter **u** stands for the same sound as _____.

the **o** in **hot**
the **u** in **but**
the **oo** in **toot**

6. In the word **chlorophyll**, the letters **ch** stand for the same sound as _____.

the **c** in **cat**
the **ch** in **chin**
the **sh** in **ship**

Name _____

Read the selection below. Try to read all the words so you can understand the selection. If you do not know a word, sound the letters and syllables and use other words in the sentences to make a good guess.

Amazing Ants

Ants, those tiny creatures that sometimes annoy us, are really very intelligent. They live together in communities where they have their own jobs as housekeepers, builders, nurses, hunters, or scouts.

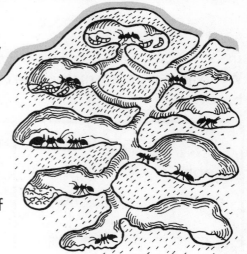

One day a naturalist (someone who studies plants and animals) observed ants carrying pieces of food back to their nest. He noticed that there always seemed to be just enough ants to carry each piece of food, no matter how small or how large it was. He wondered how that could be.

To find out, the naturalist cut a dead grasshopper into three pieces and gave each part to three scout ants. The first piece was too big for just one ant to carry. The second piece was twice as big as the first. The third piece was twice as big as the second.

The naturalist watched the three ants. Each scout ant studied its piece of food and measured it with its antennae. Then the ant went back to the nest. The ant with the smallest piece brought back twenty-eight workers to carry the food to the nest. The ant with the next larger piece brought forty-four ants, and the ant with the largest piece brought back eighty-nine worker ants. Each had brought just the right number of helpers to move its piece of the grasshopper. How the ants could solve this problem is still a mystery.

Write four difficult words on the lines below.

_____ _____ _____ _____

In this unit you will practice reading words with more unusual spellings.

Introductory teaching lesson

Name _____

The letters **ph** stand for the /**f**/ sound we hear at the beginning of **ph**one.

phone

In each box draw lines between the beginning of the word and its last syllable. Write the words on the lines. Then write the word for the picture on the line below it.

or	graph	tele	graph	alpha	phin
neph	phan	ele	phlet	dol	graph
photo	ew	pam	phants	auto	bet

_____   _____   _____

_____   _____   _____

_____   _____   _____

_____   _____   _____

Read each sentence. Choose a word from above that completes the sentence and write it on the line.

1. Dave took our _____ in front of the state capitol.

2. The _____ swam so close to me I could touch it.

3. The _____ always lead the circus parade.

4. Lian's friends wrote their names in her _____ book.

5. Mother's niece and _____ are my cousins.

6. My little sister learned the _____ from an ABC picture book.

7. The dentist gave us a _____ about taking care of our teeth.

8. Dots and dashes were used to send messages by _____.

9. After the mother bear was shot, her cub was an _____.

Name _____

Sometimes the letters **gh** stand for the /**f**/ sound. Sometimes the letters are silent.

 cou**gh**   cau**gh**t

Read each sentence below. Circle the **ough** or **augh** words.
Then circle the word in the box that rhymes with it.

1. There were enough sandwiches to feed everyone at the picnic.	new cow stuff
2. Last week Andy had a runny nose, a fever, and a bad cough.	off cow stuff
3. Mrs. Vargas taught third grade for ten years.	craft caught out
4. The tiny bird flew inside the house through the open window.	cow new off
5. Christy bought a new bike with the money she made selling hot dogs at the football games.	out caught craft
6. The wood was very rough until I rubbed it with sandpaper.	new no stuff
7. Mr. Jackson called on me because he thought I knew the answer.	craft caught out
8. I had to laugh when I heard the silly story about the clowns.	off staff law
9. Sue Lee wanted to take a plane ride although she knew it was cloudy.	no cow off

Consonant digraph: **gh** in **ough** and **augh**   **97**

Name _____

In these letter combinations, one letter is often silent.

wreath   **kn**ife   **gn**u   **gu**ard   **bu**ild   lam**b**

Read each riddle. Choose the correct word from the box and write it on the line below the riddle.

guide	building	thumb
wring	buyer	gnaw

1. someone who pays you for something

_____

2. a way to twist and squeeze out water

_____

3. a person who shows you the way

_____

4. the way a mouse might bite or chew, little by little

_____

5. a place to live or work

_____

6. the short, thick finger on your hand

_____

knit	crumbs	knee
wrap	guest	sign

7. a large poster that advertises something

_____

8. the part of the leg that bends

_____

9. something you do with yarn and long needles

_____

10. something you do to a present before you give it

_____

11. someone who is a visitor at your house

_____

12. little pieces of bread that have broken off

_____

Name _____

Choose the correct word to complete each sentence.
Circle the word and write it in the sentence.

1. Pedro has a new _____ and he is learning to play it.	guess guilty guitar
2. I asked my parents for one. They _____ it over and said I must earn the money for it.	thought enough although
3. Every day when Pedro is _____ practicing on his guitar, he lets me use it.	bought through dough
4. He shows me how to use my _____ and fingers on the strings.	knows thumb thump
5. At first my fingers felt _____ and I couldn't feel the strings very well.	numb numbers crumbs
6. Pedro told me that soon my fingers would get _____ .	laugh thought tough
7. Pedro also _____ me how to use a pick.	toast built taught
8. One day we saw a _____ advertising a guitar concert.	comb sign write
9. We went to the concert and it was super! We asked the guitar player to _____ our programs.	autograph telegraph paragraph
10. Now I know I will earn money to _____ a guitar.	guide guy buy

The letter **i** in **ild**, **ind**, and **igh** usually stands for the long **i** sound.

ch**ild**

gr**ind**

l**igh**t

The letter **o** in **old**, **olt**, and **ost** usually stands for the long **o** sound.

c**old**

c**olt**

gh**ost**

Circle the word that completes the phrase and write it on the line.

1. blind
   between
   behind

   _____ the tree

2. scout
   sight
   scold

   _____ the puppy

3. wild
   wind
   wisdom

   _____ horses

4. bright
   post
   bold

   an old fence _____

5. while
   wind
   wing

   _____ the clock

6. knight
   kind
   bright

   a _____ on horseback

7. bought
   bowl
   bolt

   a _____ of lightning

8. blindfold
   highway
   household

   a four-lane _____

Name _____

When a word ends in **all** or **alt**, the **a** stands for the sound we hear in **ball** and **salt**.

 b**all**

 s**alt**

Read each riddle. The answers have two words. In each box choose one word from the left column and one word from the right column. Write the two words on the lines below the riddle.

small	mall	tall	wall
shopping	football	salty	rainfall
steep	hall	heavy	stall
city	halter	horse	tree
leather	waterfall	stone	cracker

1. a place where a river drops from a very high point to a low point

_____ _____

2. a little ball for children to kick

_____ _____

3. a place where you can buy things in different stores

_____ _____

4. a strap used to lead a horse

_____ _____

5. a building where the mayor works

_____ _____

6. a thin, crisp snack with white specks that give it more flavor

_____ _____

7. a place in a stable for one animal

_____ _____

8. rocks that divide one plot of land from another

_____ _____

9. a long, steady rain

_____ _____

10. a green plant that reaches high into the sky

_____ _____

Reading and reasoning: sounds represented by **all**, **alt**

Name _____

When the letter **w** comes before **a** in a word, the **a** usually stands for the sound we hear in **watch** or the sound we hear in **walrus**.

 **wa**tch

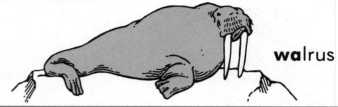 **wa**lrus

Read each riddle. Choose the correct word from the box and write it on the line below the riddle.

wasp	swallow	wallet
war	waffle	wampum

1. beads made from shells and used for money long ago

   _____

2. a flying insect that stings like a bee

   _____

3. a bird with long wings and a forked tail

   _____

4. a flat case for carrying dollar bills

   _____

5. something that looks like a large pancake

   _____

6. a time when countries are fighting

   _____

walnut	water	wand
warning	waltz	swan

7. rain, lakes, streams, and oceans all contain this

   _____

8. a large white water bird with a long neck

   _____

9. a dance done to music

   _____

10. a nut we eat that has a hard shell

    _____

11. a thin rod that a magician waves

    _____

12. something that tells us to be careful

    _____

Reading and reasoning: sounds represented by **wa**

Name _____

Choose the correct word to complete each sentence.
Circle the word and write it in the sentence.

1. Boys and girls often build snow forts in the winter. They are a common _____ in the northern part of the United States.	sigh sight size
2. Then the children choose sides for a snowball _____. An equal number of "fighters" are chosen for each side.	fight find fold
3. Each side makes a pile of snowballs. Someone always _____ everyone not to make them too hard. Snowballs can hurt!	repairs rewards reminds
4. After a while the snowball making comes to a _____, and the fight begins.	halt handle hold
5. If you get hit, you must go over to the enemy's fort. You must _____ sides.	spout stamp swap
6. You can decide to stay on that side and make up your _____ to help them win.	mold mind mitten
7. Or, you can try to escape back to your own side if you are very daring and _____. But watch out!	bold bowling burning
8. If someone hits you with a snowball as you try to escape, you _____ be sorry.	mild middle might
9. For then you must return to the enemy fort where they _____ you prisoner. You cannot try to escape again.	holler high hold
10. The fort with the _____ fighters is the winning side. Those left on the other side must raise a white flag and surrender.	misty most must

Reading sentences: letter combinations

Name _____

A SCIENCE CHALLENGE PAGE

Follow the rules you know and divide each of the science words in the boxes into syllables. When you can say a word that makes sense, write the syllables on the lines below the word. There may be more than one way to do this. Then complete each sentence with one of the words. Use a dictionary if you need help.

irrigate

_____ · _____ · _____

approximately

_____ · _____ · _____ · _ · _____ · _____

agriculture

_____ · _____ · _____ · _____

reservoir

_____ · _____ · _____

1. There is a lot of rich farm land where I live. It is easy to see that our main work

   is _____ .

2. Water for the farmers' crops comes from a

   huge _____ up in the hills.

3. This water flows down from the hills through

   pipes and ditches to _____ the fields.

4. I am not sure exactly how big the reservoir

   is. But I think it is _____ 20 miles long.

accurate

_____ · _____ · _____

pollute

_____ · _____

average

_____ · _____ · _____

analyze

_____ · _ · _____

5. Sometimes people use the reservoir for boating and fishing. They must be careful

   not to _____ the water.

6. The water is tested each month. Scientists

   _____ it to tell if it is all right for food crops.

7. They also take careful and _____ measurements of the rainfall each year.

8. Then they can figure out what the

   _____ rainfall is every five or ten years.

Name _____

A SOCIAL STUDIES CHALLENGE PAGE

Follow the rules you know and divide each of the social studies words in the boxes into syllables. When you can say a word that makes sense, write the syllables on the lines below the word. There may be more than one way to do this. Then complete each sentence with one of the words. Use a dictionary if you need help.

volunteers

_____ . ___ . _____

citizens

_____ . _ . _____

immigrant

___ . ___ . _____

neighborhood

_____ . ___ . _____

1. My mother was born in Cuba. She is an

_____ to the United States.

2. The people who live next door came from Korea five years ago. Now they are

_____ of the United States.

3. The people in our _____ come from many different countries.

4. Many people help the teachers once a week. They are school _____.

commuters

_____ . ___ . _____

manufacture

_____ . _ . _____ . _____

community

_____ . ___ . ___ . _____

census

_____ . _____

5. In class we are studying about our city. It is a very large _____.

6. Two million people living in our city were counted in the _____ last year.

7. Each day many people come by train or car to work here. They are _____.

8. Two companies in our city

_____ parts for cars.

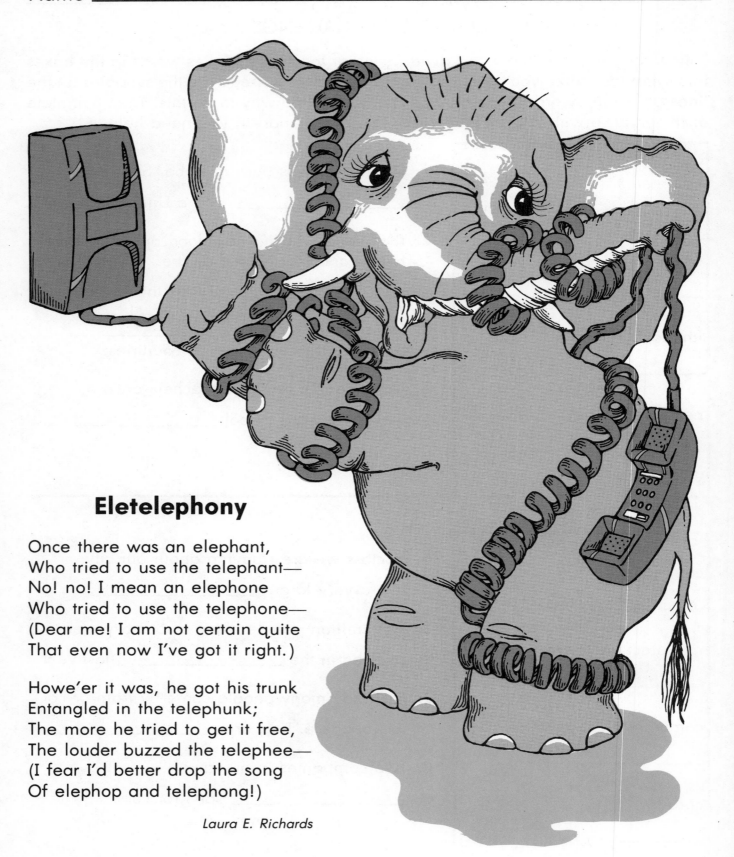

Eletelephony

Once there was an elephant,
Who tried to use the telephant—
No! no! I mean an elephone
Who tried to use the telephone—
(Dear me! I am not certain quite
That even now I've got it right.)

Howe'er it was, he got his trunk
Entangled in the telephunk;
The more he tried to get it free,
The louder buzzed the telephee—
(I fear I'd better drop the song
Of elephop and telephong!)

Laura E. Richards

Name _____

Read the story. Circle the words to complete the sentences.
Write the words in the sentences.

1. One day I was out walking in the field in back of my aunt's house. A honking noise startled me, and I looked up to see an amazing _____ .	wrist blind sight
2. A small flock of _____ geese was flying overhead in the shape of the letter V.	wren wild gnaw
3. I _____ as the bird in the lead turned and headed toward the field. Then as the flock followed it down, I had my eye on another bird.	wallop watched squall
4. I had to _____ as it rolled over on its back in flight, but its head didn't turn over. I never expected to see that strange sight.	laugh rough dough
5. Geese keep their heads _____ even when they fly upside down. This keeps them from getting mixed up about the direction in which they are going.	upright buying midnight
6. I _____ that was pretty funny. Then I remembered that sometimes I had to turn a roadmap upside down to know if I would make a left or right turn.	cough thought through
7. The geese all landed right side up in the field. Every neck was stretched to its full _____ . Every bird was listening for any strange sounds.	height high taught

8. Finding it safe, the leader gave a _____ and the geese began to feed. All, that is, except one who remained with its neck erect.	signal design limb
9. That bird acted as the lookout and did not eat. Its job was to _____ the flock and warn of any danger.	guard guess guest
10. I had read about this, but now I was close _____ to observe it. Soon another goose took over as guard and the first guard had its chance to eat.	tough enough remind
11. The goose on guard did not seem to mind when I went closer to take _____ of these handsome birds. This was my lucky day!	photos phrases flight

Write a story about your
favorite birds.

_____

_____

_____

_____

_____

_____

_____

_____

_____

TALES

FROM AROUND THE WORLD

1

Daylight Comes at Last

It was the time of endless night, and Raven set out to see what he could find. Bumping through the forest, Raven felt his way blindly through the darkness.

Suddenly a shimmer of brilliant light flashed among the trees. Raven folded his wings and crept cautiously to find out what was going on. Then, where the trees meet the water, Raven found his old friend, Sea Gull. Sea Gull was so busy shutting a box that he didn't notice Raven.

"What is it you have in your box?" asked Raven, surprising his friend.

Sea Gull reached under his bed and snatched the hidden box. "Here," he moaned. "I'll give you a little light," and he opened the box a crack.

"Such big thorns!" exclaimed Raven, pulling out one, two, three. "But these little ones, I can see them hardly at all."

Groaning loudly, Sea Gull opened the box a little wider.

Raven picked and picked. "One more to go," he breathed. "Give me a little more light."

This time when Sea Gull reached for the box, Raven gave Sea Gull a little shove. The box fell open wide and all the daylight escaped. Light flooded every corner of the house. It spread outside, down the path, shimmering across the water and over the hills.

"Come back! Come back!" shouted Sea Gull to his escaping treasure. He flew out the door, racing across the hills to gather back his precious Daylight. But it was too late. Daylight was spreading across the world, coming at last to all the people.

Raven had to listen to Sea Gull's loud complaints as long as Daylight glowed. But when Daylight traveled on to the other side of the world and night came, Sea Gull yawned and fell asleep. Then Raven slipped into the forest to see what else he could find.

4

"Nothing much," snapped Sea Gull. But the way he hurried off with his box made Raven certain that it held a treasure.

Raven decided to stay near Sea Gull's lodge to try to find out more. Soon Raven heard Sea Gull mumbling and fumbling in the dark. Raven crept to the door of the lodge and peered in. Sea Gull was doing something with his box. He opened the lid a little crack. Suddenly the lodge was flooded with light! Raven could see everything in the lodge and every feather on Sea Gull's head. Raven crouched in the dark and watched Sea Gull work about his lodge without a stumble or a bump.

"What a treasure Sea Gull has!" thought Raven. "Everyone should have this thing." But when Sea Gull was ready to sleep, Raven watched him snap down the lid of the box firmly. He shut the light back inside it, before hiding the box under his bed. "That selfish Sea Gull wants to keep his treasure all to himself," thought Raven. "Let's see what I can do to make him share it!"

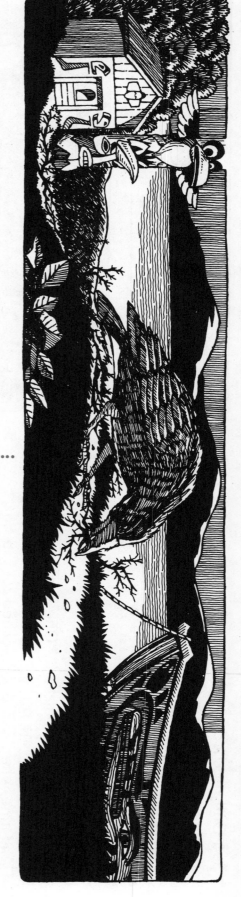

While Sea Gull slept, Raven clipped hawthorn branches from the trees around Sea Gull's lodge. Carefully, so that the long thorns wouldn't scratch him, Raven laid the branches along the path from Sea Gull's lodge to the water's edge. He covered the path down to the place where Sea Gull's canoe was fastened to a stump. Then Raven untied the rope and set the canoe adrift.

"Sea Gull! Sea Gull!" shouted Raven as the canoe drifted away with the current. "Your boat is floating off! Hurry!"

Sea Gull leaped from his sleep. He bumped through his doorway and bounded down the path. "OUCH! Oh! Ouch, ouch!" screeched Sea Gull. He jumped from one leg to the other right back to his house. "Raven, save my boat! My feet are full of thorns," cried Sea Gull.

When Raven had brought back the canoe, he found Sea Gull picking the thorns from his feet.

"Let me help you," offered Raven. "How I wish I could see better to help my old friend!"

Name _____

Listen to each word. Find the word in the box and circle it.

1.	2.	3.	4.	5.
though	parent	fog	laugh	roost
tough	falcon	fight	launch	rough
thought	phantom	fit	law	roam
through	pattern	fought	leave	round

6.	7.	8.	9.	10.
cover	never	though	paragraph	enforce
knock	nephew	tough	private	entire
cough	navigate	through	proof	enjoy
cove	nightfall	thought	parallel	enough

11.	12.	13.	14.	15.
white	kind	gnat	galley	boom
roast	kitty	gate	guilty	bone
write	nutty	gang	gull	bomb
rate	knotty	night	gill	born

16.	17.	18.	19.	20.
bulb	mail	find	brace	foil
built	milk	finger	bright	fond
bugle	mild	finch	braid	fled
burst	mill	fins	broth	fold

21.	22.	23.	24.	25.
joint	must	insult	salt	whale
jewel	most	instead	sold	wolf
jot	mast	install	self	wobble
jolt	mist	involve	silt	wallop

Review for Unit 8   **111**

Name _____

Read the selection below. Try to read all the words so you can understand the selection. If you do not know a word, sound the letters and syllables and use other words in the sentences to make a good guess.

Clever Elephants

Elephants are very intelligent animals. They can easily learn thirty or forty spoken commands, such as "lift your foot" and "kneel." They also do some very intelligent things without commands.

For instance, an elephant can clear trees on its own. The trainer points out an area, and the elephant uproots the trees, one by one. The elephant uses its head to push a tree until it leans. Then it uses its foot to shove the tree to the ground. If roots keep the tree from falling, the elephant will walk around the tree and pull out the roots, without being told.

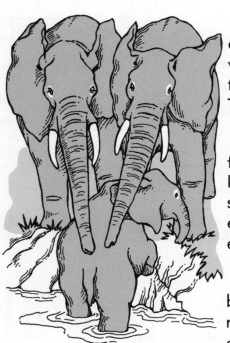

Two big elephants once rescued a helpless young elephant without any commands. The young elephant was trapped in a very deep mud hole. The big elephants trampled down the sides of the hole to form a ramp. Then they pulled the young elephant out to safety.

Elephants respond to kindness and understanding from their trainers. Perhaps that is because they are kind to each other in the wild. A mother elephant shows affection, but she often spanks her young elephant with her trunk if it disobeys. A young elephant stays with its mother for sixteen years.

Circus elephants also learn many things. They can balance on a rolling ball, perform on a seesaw, or ride bicycles. Wherever they are, elephants show great intelligence.

Write four difficult words on the lines below.

_____ _____ _____ _____

In this unit you will practice reading words with prefixes and suffixes.

Name _____

The prefixes **un**, **dis**, **im**, and **in** are syllables that mean **not** or **to do the opposite of**. You can add these prefixes to the beginning of base words to make new words with different meanings.

un + balanced
unbalanced
not balanced

im + perfect
imperfect
not perfect

dis + connect
disconnect
opposite of connect

in + correct
incorrect
not correct

Divide each word below into syllables.
Remember: The first syllable in these words is the prefix.

impossible ___ ____ ___ ____   disloyal ____ ____ ___

disagree ____ _____   unbutton __ __ ____

impolite __ __ ____   inexpensive __ __ ____ _____

inactive ___ ___ ____   unbuckle __ ____ ___

Read each sentence. Choose a word from above that completes the sentence and write it on the line.

1. That man was _____ when he gave secrets to the enemy.

2. The smallest child needed someone to help him _____ his sweater.

3. I had to _____ with Amelia because I knew she was wrong.

4. Mother told us that we must not _____ our seatbelts.

5. Bears do not really hibernate, but they are _____ during the winter months.

6. My bike did not cost much. It was _____ because it needed a new wheel.

7. Look at that steep cliff. It seems _____ for anyone to climb it.

8. It is _____ to rush to the head of the bus line.

Negative prefixes: **un, dis, im, in**

Name _____

The prefix **mis** often means **wrong**.

    mis + spelled = misspelled

        spelled wrong

bicicle

The prefix **pre** often means **before**.

    pre + paid = prepaid

        paid before or ahead

The prefix **re** often means **back** or **again**.

    re + grew = regrew

        grew back or grew again

Divide each word below into syllables.

Remember: The first syllable in these words is the prefix.

reappear   ___ ___ _____   preview   ____ _____

misjudged   _____ _____   mispronounce   _____ ____ _____

renamed   ___ _____   misplace   ____ _____

retrace   ___ _____   repainted   ___ _____ ___

Read each sentence. Choose a word from above that completes the sentence and write it on the line.

1. I cannot find my book. I seem to _____ it all the time.

2. Mr. Alvirez _____ the distance between the car fender and the garage door and scratched his car.

3. The bench is scratched and needs to be _____ .

4. Before the class saw the film, Lin Su and I had a chance to _____ it.

5. We watched the plane _____ on the other side of the cloud.

6. The word *soldier* is hard to spell, and I often _____ it also.

7. If we leave markers along our trail, it will be easy to _____ our steps.

8. The Idlewild Airport in New York was _____ for President John F. Kennedy.

Name _____

Read each definition. Choose the correct word from the box above it and write the word on the line below its definition.

impatient	uncommon
mistreat	disappear
preview	rearrange
unselfish	

1. to go out of sight

_____

2. restless

_____

3. to see ahead

_____

4. unusual, not ordinary

_____

5. to treat badly

_____

6. not selfish

_____

7. to arrange again

_____

recount	dishonest
misunderstood	impolite
unwrapped	indefinite
reuse	

8. not truthful

_____

9. count again

_____

10. not understood

_____

11. not clear or definite

_____

12. not showing good manners

_____

13. to use again

_____

14. not wrapped

_____

Name _____

A suffix is a syllable that has a meaning and comes at the end of a word.

The suffix **ful** means **full of**.

pain + **ful**
painful
full of pain

The suffix **ly** means **in that way**.

slow + **ly**
slowly
in a slow way

The suffix **less** means **without**.

home + **less**
homeless
without a home

The suffix **ness** means **being**.

dark + **ness**
darkness
being dark

Divide each word below into syllables. The last syllable is the suffix.

delightful _____ _____ _____   cleverly _____ _____ _____

breathless _____ _____   worthless _____ _____

cleverness _____ _____ _____   successful _____ _____ _____

foolishly _____ _____ _____   sweetness _____ _____

Read each sentence. Choose a word from above that completes the sentence and write it on the line.

1. We had a very _____ science fair at school this year. Many of us won prizes.

2. Amanda _____ left the tiny plants she was growing outdoors, and they froze. She did not win a prize.

3. Maria's drawings of mushrooms were _____ .

4. Corey's test for _____ showed the amount of sugar in candy.

5. Then he _____ compared them all on a big bar graph.

6. Corey's _____ helped our class take first place.

7. Carlos's experiment was _____ after his cat upset a pan of earthworms.

8. Ellen was _____ after running for an hour and keeping a careful record of her heartbeat rate.

Name _____

The suffix **er** often means
a person who or **something that**.

sharpen **+ er**
= sharpener
something that sharpens

The suffix **or** often means
a person who or **something that**.

act **+ or** = actor
a person who acts

When you add **er** or **or** to a base word that ends in **e**, first drop the **e**. Keep the long sound of the first vowel.

glide **+ er** = glider

When you add **er** or **or** to a short vowel word (CVC), first double the final consonant. Keep the short sound of the first vowel.

rob **+ er** = robber

Read each word and write it under the correct picture.

explorer
shopper
teacher
driver

_____ _____ _____ _____

collector
operator
conductor
visitor

_____ _____ _____ _____

Read each sentence. Write a word from above to complete the sentence.

1. My dad is a _____ of old coins.

2. Mrs. Weller asked the taxi cab _____ to take her to the library.

3. The _____ used a cart at the supermarket.

4. The crane _____ moved the huge steel beams.

5. The _____ Christopher Columbus discovered a new world.

6. Mrs. Curtin, the _____ of our school band, made us work very hard, but it was fun.

Suffixes: **er, or** **117**

Name _____

The suffix **ment** means the **result of an action** or **state of**.
It changes an action word to a word that names something.

announce + **ment** = announcement
When you announce something,
you make an announcement.

The suffix **en** sometimes means **made of** and sometimes **to make**.

wood + **en** = wooden
made of wood

short + **en** = shorten
to make shorter

Read each word and write it under the correct picture.

agreement
payment
shipment
arrangement

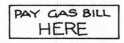

_____ _____ _____ _____

sweeten
woolen
golden
flatten

_____ _____ _____ _____

Read each sentence. Write a word from above to complete the sentence.

1. Mrs. Okada carefully placed the tall flowers in the vase to make a beautiful

   _____ .

2. My _____ cap is warmer than your cotton one.

3. Our car is paid for. Dad made the last _____ today.

4. These _____ rings are brighter than the silver ones.

5. To recycle metal cans, step on them and _____ them.

6. The workers helped load a big _____ of wheat onto the boat.

7. Many countries signed the _____ to stop hunting whales.

8. Should I use more sugar to _____ the lemonade?

Name _____

The suffix **ion** means **act** or **result of**.
When you add the suffix **ion** to an action word, it changes to a word that names something.

elect + **ion** = election   decorate + **ion** = decoration
e·lec·tion   dec·or·a·tion

Add the suffix **ion** to the following words. Then divide the new words into syllables.

direct + ion = _____   migrate + ion = _____

___ ___ ___   ___ ___ ___

locate + ion = _____   rotate + ion = _____

___ ___ ___   ___ ___ ___

pollute + ion = _____   inspect + ion = _____

___ ___ ___   ___ ___ ___

Read each sentence. Choose a base word or a word with a suffix from above and write it on the line.

1. Every spring the geese _____ from down south to Canada. They always stop in Mr. Zinna's field.

2. They stay for a few days, feeding in the field and nearby river. Then they always fly off in the same _____.

3. Mr. Zinna is careful about the insect spray he uses on his crops. He does not want to _____ the river.

4. Water _____ could kill the geese and other birds. It could also harm Mr. Zinna's crops.

5. Mr. Zinna is a wise farmer. Every year he changes the _____ of his crops.

6. Sometimes farmers move their crops around, or rotate them, to different fields. This is called crop _____.

7. Rotating crops is good for the soil and helps get rid of insects. An _____ of Mr. Zinna's field proves this.

8. Mr. Zinna cares about the _____ of geese, and he cares about the growing of crops.

      Suffix: **ion**   **119**

Name _____

The suffixes **able** and **ible** often mean **can be done**.

 sink + **able**
sinkable
can be sunk

 reverse + **ible**
reversible
can be reversed

Read the words below. Figure out each base word and write it on the line.

avoidable _____

passable _____

movable _____

huggable _____

readable _____

collapsible _____

convertible _____

excusable _____

Read each sentence. Choose a base word or a word with a suffix from above to complete each sentence. Write the word on the line.

1. Even Sara's oldest brother thought her new teddy bear was

_____ .

2. The bridge washed out during the storm. Now it is no longer

_____ .

3. Three heavy logs blocked the road, and the men could not

_____ them.

4. The umbrella collapses and folds into a short tube. It is _____ .

5. The workers tied the ten ropes carefully so the tent would not

_____ on the animals.

6. Mr. Dean pressed a button and the top of his car went back into the trunk. He has

a _____ car.

7. Mrs. Torres would not _____ Cindy from the gym class.

8. The print under the pictures was too small to be _____ .

9. Even the best driver could not avoid that accident. It was not

_____ .

10. If she got only one more correct answer, she would _____
the test.

Name _____

Choose the correct word to complete each sentence.
Circle the word and write it in the sentence.

1. Today my dog, Buster, and I finish dog training school.
   We have both shown great _____.

   improvement
   disorder
   inspection

2. Let me give you some of the most _____
   hints I have learned about training dogs.

   harmful
   youthful
   helpful

3. Do not play with your dog while you are training him. Be
   stern and act like a _____.

   inventor
   trainer
   shopper

4. Do not work with your dog too long or when it is too hot.
   Try to keep your dog _____.

   comfortable
   forgettable
   useless

5. Be careful to use the same words for commands. Don't be
   _____ and say "Come" one day and
   "Come over here" another day.

   unselfish
   careless
   unbroken

6. If you keep your dog's work interesting, he will look
   forward to the training session _____.

   eagerly
   slowly
   sickly

7. When your dog follows your _____, reward
   him with praise and patting, not food.

   leader
   mistrust
   directions

8. Do not strike your dog. Show _____ and try
   to understand him.

   distrust
   nervousness
   kindness

9. Do not _____ your dog. If you lose your
   temper during training, stop until you feel better.

   shorten
   frighten
   refill

10. Praise will work better than _____ as you
    and your dog work together.

    infection
    payment
    punishment

Reading sentences: suffixes **121**

Name _____

First divide longer words between the prefix (or suffix) and the base word. Then, if you do not know the base word, divide it into syllables.

Words can have more than one prefix or suffix.

They can have a prefix and a suffix.   They can have several suffixes.

unfriendly = un + friend **+ ly**   **hopelessness** = hope **+ less + ness**

        not like a friend   being without hope

Write the base word for each of the words in the boxes. Then write the correct word in each sentence.

disagreement _____
unsuccessful _____
uncomfortable _____
impatiently _____

1. It was getting late. Bart and I waited _____ to try out for a part in the class play.

2. I was _____ because I was hungry and tired of waiting to read for the part.

3. Bart and I both wanted the part of the old pirate. We had a _____ about how mean and gruff he should be.

4. Both of us read for the part, but Mrs. Martin gave Bart a second chance to read. He got the part. I was _____ .

unfairly _____
unforgettable _____
replacement _____
thankfully _____

5. This morning Bart fell and broke his leg. Now they will have to find a _____ for him.

6. Although I feel I was treated a bit _____ yesterday, I still want the part.

7. Two other boys wanted the part. But, _____ , I got it this time.

8. Learning the part means lots of practice. But I know it will be an _____ time.

Name _____

Read the story. Circle the words to complete the sentences.
Write the words in the sentences.

1. The empty lot next to our school belongs to the city. Some people dump their trash there. It is a _____ sight.	disagreement disgraceful development
2. The students made a _____ to the principal. We asked her if we could have a playground there.	suggestion amazement inventor
3. Our principal liked the idea, and she called Mayor Stennis. The mayor sent out an _____ to look at the lot.	invention inspector pitcher
4. A week later the mayor met with our principal. There was great _____ at school.	direction forgetfulness excitement
5. The mayor said the city did not have enough money for such an expensive project. He was sorry, but he was _____ to help us.	unthankful harmlessly unable
6. We wouldn't take "No" for an answer. We _____ set to work ourselves. Many kids and parents spent a lot of time getting rid of all the junk in the lot.	cheerfully hopelessly cheeriness
7. Then the PTA held a flea market to earn money. They raised the _____ sum of $9,000.	teachable unbelievable vacation

Reading a story and expressive writing **123**

8. The kids held a car wash every Saturday and earned $1,000 more. The $10,000 was enough to pay for the playground _____.	wasteful dictator equipment
9. Then our principal went back to the mayor and asked if the city could pay for just the _____ work.	construction jobless breakable
10. The mayor came out to see what had been done to the lot. He looked at it in _____. Mayor Stennis promised the city would pay for the work.	arrangement amazement invention
11. The kids promised to keep the playground clean. Soon everything was done. We had a big _____ and asked the mayor to open our new playground.	pollution division celebration

Write a story about working
together on a project.

_____

_____

_____

_____

_____

_____

_____

_____

Boo's World

Spring

Boo is a three-day-old caribou calf—and already he can run. The best way for a newborn caribou to escape hungry enemies is to be on its feet, and on the move—quickly.

Boo's world is the tundra of northern Canada—a flat, windswept world without trees. A snowstorm during the last week of May is not unusual. It snowed the day Boo was born.

Boo's mother gives him all her attention and all her milk. It is rich milk. Boo is a big eater, and he is growing rapidly.

As he grows he runs. He runs everywhere and explores the world around him.

To the three-day-old caribou calf, Mom's licks mean all is okay.

Summer

It is now early summer, and the tundra is covered with juicy grasses, low leafy shrubs, brightly colored wildflowers, and other plants. Soon the young caribou is nibbling at the tundra plants. Now and then he eats a mushroom. But Boo's favorite food is lichens.

Lichens are simple plants that grow thick on the tundra. They have no flowers or leaves. One kind, called "reindeer moss," is a favorite food for reindeer and caribou.

Lichens grow very slowly. Once they have been nibbled off, it takes a long time for them to grow back. That is why caribou herds are always on the move, searching for plants that are big enough to eat. So each morning, Boo's herd wakes up in a different place. It is good that Boo likes to run and has strong legs.

Boo's feet are very large and wide—perfect for tundra travel. The tundra is often wet, and his large spreading feet help keep Boo from sinking into the soggy ground.

Boo's world is soft and swampy and has many lakes and rivers. And just as Boo's big feet help

Boo's large spreading feet are good for travel on the soggy tundra.

him walk, they also make great paddles and help him swim. His hair helps too. Each hair is hollow and filled with air. When Boo swims across a river, his coat helps keep him afloat, like a life jacket.

The herd grows larger through the summer. Male caribou with huge towering antlers join the mothers and calves. Boo's herd has met other herds. And soon there are thousands of animals, a sea of caribou stretching across the tundra.

Finally August comes, and the giant herd breaks up into small herds again. The caribou walk, they eat, they rest. But one day it snows. The season is turning.

Boo is beginning to grow a new coat. His baby coat is falling out in patches. When he walks through bushes, it snags and pulls away. Soon Boo's coat is the same gray-tan color as the older caribou.

At the same time, something else is growing. Boo's first set of antlers sprout from his head!

Fall

One morning Boo's herd begins a long journey—their fall migration. Boo and his mother walk with the herd for many days, always heading in the same direction. This is Boo's first migration. He will learn the way to the southern edge of the tundra. There they will spend the winter, where food will be easier to find. And he will learn the way back in spring.

Boo walks south with the herd for many days.

In the spring, the females will lead the march back to the tundra. There they will give birth to new calves. Older calves like Boo will be on their own. It is the same year after year. It is the way of the caribou, the way of Boo's world.

 Bookshelf

These books will tell you more about caribou.

Harris, Lorie K. *The Caribou.* Minneapolis, Minn.: Dillion Press, 1988.

Owens, Mary B. *A Caribou Alphabet.* Gardiner, Me.: Dog Ear Press, 1988.

The Library

It looks like any building
When you pass it on the street,
Made of stone and glass and marble,
Made of iron and concrete.

But once inside you can ride
A camel or a train,
Visit Rome, Siam, or Nome,
Feel a hurricane,
Meet a king, learn to sing,
How to bake a pie,
Go to sea, plant a tree,
Find how airplanes fly,
Train a horse, and of course
Have all the dogs you'd like,
See the moon, a sandy dune,
Or catch a whopping pike.
Everything that books can bring
You'll find inside those walls.
A world is there for you to share
When adventure calls.

You cannot tell its magic
By the way the building looks,
But there's wonderment within it,
The wonderment of books.

Barbara A. Huff

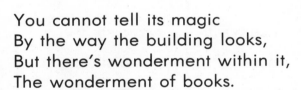

Name _____

Listen to the sentence. Find the word in the box and circle it.

1.	2.	3.	4.
fearful	completely	imperfect	honestly
unafraid	incomplete	perfectly	dishonest

5.	6.	7.	8.
rewrite	preview	untreated	unpainted
written	review	mistreated	repainted

9.	10.	11.	12.
pointless	director	undecided	forceless
pointer	direction	decision	forcible

13.	14.	15.	16.
usable	actor	announcement	moisten
useless	action	announcer	moistless

17.	18.	19.	20.
politeness	unfree	restless	hopeless
impolite	freely	restful	hopeful

21.	22.	23.	24.
carefully	unfriendly	orderliness	removable
carelessness	friendliness	disorderly	immovable